Praise for **The Wrong Side of** (

When she was done speaking at a conference I attended, I really wanted to "be" her. I was drawn to her confidence and inspired by her persistence. Mostly I was struck by the personal sacrifice she made—giving up a career, suspending her personal life, starving herself down to "pro weight material"— for a shot at greatness. She has something special and it conveys.

—Theresa Urban, CEO
1406 Group, Arlington, VA

A great leader is never forgotten and Amy Charity is hard to forget. The most important characteristics of a great Coach and/or Leader are that they are knowledgeable of the sport, have patience, can motivate and is a good communicator. Amy possesses all of these important characteristics in addition to deeply caring about people. She has high personal standards and ambitions that are easily translated to motivate others.

—Dianna Anderson, Chief Data Officer
State of Colorado, Denver, CO

Inspiration Guaranteed! Amy is a well versed, personable speaker. She is engaging and motivating and delivers an energetic and entertaining approach to coaching and speaking. Her simple concepts that focus on creating a positive mindset that will dictate successful outcomes resonated with everyone. Truly inspiring!

—Lynda Edoff, teacher
Tucson, AZ

Amy brings her pro cycling experience to training, along with superior character and motivation. Amy has demonstrated her ability to motivate athletes at all levels on the triathlon team. She treats all athletes as teammates spending time coaching and encouraging all riders. Her knowledge of training methods, technique, and performance potential has encouraged all team members to push their limits to achieve goals not previously recognized. I have definitely benefited from Amy's dedication and spirit.

—Deb Rose, head coach
SSWSC Cross Country, Steamboat Springs, CO

Amy is every bit as inspiring a person as she is an incredible rider on the bike. She will humbly tear your legs off on a hard climb or a 150 mile ride and then offer encouragement when you beg for mercy. An incredible talent on the bike who seems to thrive the longer the ride goes on or the higher the mountain ascends into the clouds. Amy is an equally fun to spend time with off the bike, and with prodding she will humbly regale with stories of riding the entirety of the Tour de France route in three weeks or racing in the UCI World Championships or earning the privilege of wearing the Stars and Stripes by winning the USA National Championships. Her passion and love of the sport really shine through with everything she does.

—Kyle Yost, entrepreneur
Washington DC

Amy's story is a model for everyone to follow. She is driven, intelligent and an extremely hard worker. All keys to success in sport and in life.

—Eric Kenney, coach
Boulder, CO

Amy's life experience and smarts made her a fierce competitor because even in the most challenging times in a race, she knew she chose to be there. Being overqualified for bike racing made her have the ability to embrace the sport for the pure passion of it. This made her an inspiring teammate with contagious enthusiasm and dedication to mastering a skill, because why not?

—Alison Tetrick, Professional Cyclist
Petaluma, CA

"I first met Amy when I treated her for a musculoskeletal injury during Ironman training. In the years that I have known her since what has always struck me about Amy is her ability to stay positive and work hard to overcome the challenges laid before her. She got fit for the ironman, only to break her collar bone weeks before the race. She accepted her fate, refocused, rehabilitated and bounced back to complete Ironman Switzerland in a super time and with a super attitude."

—Andy Proffitt, Physical Therapist
Felixstowe, England

After knowing Amy Charity for 12 years and watching her many sacrifices to compete in the cycling world professionally, it was a thrill to see her do an equally professional job as a speaker. In July of 2017, she addressed a mixed-age group with a wide variety of backgrounds at Steamboat Springs High School and you could have heard a pin drop. As a writer and public speaker myself, I respect Amy's abilities in both arenas as a way to bring her inspirational message to broad audiences. Her many experiences, and dedication to helping others succeed, contribute to her unique ability to coach others who are willing to "do what it takes" to reach their goals.

—Susan E. Mead, Essentrics Instructor,
Medical Herbalist and author of award-winning *Take Back Your Body,*
Steamboat Springs, Colorado

The Wrong Side of Comfortable

Chase your dream.
Discover your potential.
Transform your life.

Amy Charity

Cover photography: George Fargo, George Fargo Photography
Book Consultant: Judith Briles, The Book Shepherd
Cover and interior design: Rebecca Finkel, F + P Graphic Design
eBook conversion: Rebecca Finkel, F + P Graphic Design

ISBN print: 978-0-9992246-0-1
ISBN eBook: 978-0-9992246-1-8

Library of Congress Control Number: 2017949405
Inspiration | Memoir | Cycling |S elf-Help

First Edition
Printed in the USA

To my parents,

for instilling the belief in me

that anything is possible

and for unwavering love

every step of the way.

Contents

**Live life
without
regrets.**

*And in the end, it's not
the years in your life that count.
It's the life in your years.*
—Abraham Lincoln

PART I

Unlocking Possibilities.
The Why.
Your Purpose

CHAPTER ONE

Am I Still Breathing?

My vision began to narrow.
Just keep pedaling,
Amy—just stay on his wheel,
I told myself.

Realization Point Trailhead (Boulder, CO)

I could not have known at the time. I could not have fully understood, or even accepted the magnitude of the situation, or the symbolism of the sign that I was leaning against. As I stood, bent over my bike, heaving, my bodily functions not within my immediate control, I peered at the sign with my vision just coming back. It said: Realization Point Trailhead.

Sixteen minutes and three seconds had separated me from the bottom of Flagstaff Road where I had begun the ascent, riding immediately behind my coach's wheel. He had warned me that the ride was going to be difficult.

How could 16 minutes hurt that much? I wondered. I can do anything for 16 minutes.

The objectives were clear. My coach knew that I was a decent climber, and he wanted to test my desire and my drive. I had the arbitrary goal of reaching the top of one of Boulder's most well-known climbs in under 16 minutes—breaking the 'known' existing female record.. Achieving this goal would serve as an indication that I could be considered one of the best female climbers in a highly competitive town of world class cyclists.

Jeff's instructions were also clear: *"I'm going to pace you to the top of the climb. Stay right on my wheel. I will have you above your threshold, so this is going to hurt. Just stay on my wheel."*

Following his directions, the first three minutes flew by and pedaling actually felt easy. The town of Boulder quickly appeared below the road and our perspective of the city increased as the grade of the road steepened. I was intimately familiar with the stages of my heart rate increases from previous athletic endeavors.

I looked down at my bike computer, and we were already five minutes into the climb. Passing a few other cyclists on the road, I muttered a grunt that came out as less than a hello. My breathing shifted to fast panting, and I could no longer speak. Nine minutes had now passed. At that point, my heartrate was in the mid-160s.

The pain in my heart, legs, lungs, and head was indescribable.

It started to feel uncomfortable. I wanted to back off the pedals, just slightly, to ease the discomfort building in my legs and my lungs. My Garmin now tells me that 12 minutes have ticked by. Uh-oh, the familiar little cough has started—a cough that I can't control. I heard its desperate sound—a warning—and knew, without looking, that my heart rate had reached the 180s. Uh-oh, it's all over soon, I thought. I hope it's the top of the hill that puts this to an end and not my body.

I knew my mind wouldn't give up ... that I would keep pedaling until I passed out. Of course, I hoped that the top would come first. I looked down and saw 15 minutes on the Garmin. OMG, I was losing my senses. The pain in my heart, legs, lungs, and head was indescribable. I couldn't say what was hurting, but I knew the lights would be turning out for me soon. My vision began to narrow. Just keep pedaling, Amy—just stay on his wheel, I told myself.

The familiar wheezing had begun, the high-pitched sound that I couldn't replicate unless I was in that state of fighting for breath. My heart rate was now in the 190s. I knew I was down to the final seconds before my body would stop.

I made it to the top and couldn't speak. I couldn't stand upright. I lost control of bodily functions. "Did I do it?" I finally asked, feebly. "Did I break the record for fastest women's time up Flagstaff?"

"I think you might have been three seconds off the record. Don't worry, we'll get you there," Jeff responded cautiously, understanding how badly I wanted to prove to myself that I could do it, that I was one of the best female climbers in the state.

As I stood at Realization Point Trailhead, having completed one of the most challenging physical efforts of my life, the subtle realization dawned on me. Nothing about achieving my cycling goals would come easy. In a training session, I experienced a deeper level of suffering than I had previously known—I had just been categorically and unquestionably on the wrong side of comfortable, and still had not achieved my immediate goal of riding to the top in under 16 minutes.

As I stood over my bike, leaning against the trailhead sign, heaving, sweating, shivering, I realized that I was embarking on a journey of suffering, to degrees that I never could have imagined. Somehow, even at that moment, I realized I was on the right path. My passion for cycling, my curiosity of where I could take my cycling career, and my drive to be a world class competitor outweighed everything.

MENTAL STATE: *This already hurts and I've only just begun.*

This is going to hurt.

To experience anything worthwhile, you will cross over the line to the wrong side of comfortable.

BOTTOM LINE: almost anything in your life that is worthwhile requires hard work, desire, determination, and the courage to overcome challenges. These challenges may be mental, physical, financial, or emotional. My hope is that my journey inspires you to take the plunge, step out of your comfort zone, and confidently make life choices leading to a life of fulfillment and without regret. While you will be on the wrong side of comfortable, you will be in a place of learning and growing and living your life to your potential.

take away

Learning Zone

Comfort Zone

CHAPTER TWO

It's Not Too Late

Prior to jumping off my own cliff of life as I knew it, I had a notion of the "ideal" timing to taking risks and making major life changes. I would have suggested that the "appropriate" occasion would be any of the following: between jobs, right after college, during my 20s, after a relationship ends, immediately before or after a move. In my case, my timing to pursue a career as a cyclist defied all stereotypical norms.

1 I was in my mid-30s

2 I was married

3 I had a solid group of tight-knit friends

4 I passionately loved where I lived

5 I had an incredible job with a promising future

6 I loved my life

Regardless of suboptimal timing, I knew I had to do it. I knew that I had to risk losing all of the above (with the exception of my age!) to pursue the life of a bike racer (in spite of my age!).

While age is not necessarily a physical hindrance in an endurance sport such as bike racing, my life stage versus those of my teammates was noteworthy. The average age of women in the professional cycling peloton is twenty-five. Still in their twenties, these young women had not yet acquired many bulky possessions, such as the occasional couch, dresser, or television, or car (!) and therefore could store their belongings at their parents' houses.

It was simply a continuation of college life, except better.

Few owned their own home, and if they had made the move away from their parents, they shared apartments with friends or teammates. Most of these women were single and therefore did not find themselves in the heart-wrenching discussion about what it might mean for the future of their marriage if they decided to pursue a career of bike racing. It was so rare to be married in the Pro Peloton that my husband started referring to me as #ProWife and the name stuck! When calling my attention, teammates would say "Hey, Amy, Pro Wife!"

A poverty-level salary was not a showstopper for these young women, either. As these millennial women had recently graduated from college, the idea of surviving on little to no salary seemed somewhat normal. It was simply a continuation of college life, except better. They would be given bikes, cycling kits, plane tickets to race, and would make a few thousand dollars in prize money (racing prime, see page 204 for definition). What more could one (in her twenties!) possibly need?

I had a dream, drive, and the will to give it a shot.

My situation was different on all accounts. Thirty-four years old, married, homeowner in a magical mountain resort town, fifteen-year career in financial services and investments, devoted "mom" to a Boxador named Lucy, strong network of active and outdoor-loving friends, I was not an ideal candidate for a major life change.

I left my job, my husband (temporarily), my home, and my life in Steamboat Springs, Colorado to pursue my dream of racing bikes professionally at the age of thirty-four. I did not take this decision lightly. I was not independently wealthy. It was crystal-clear that my husband and I would make many financial sacrifices. I had no guarantees that any of my plans would be realized. I had a dream, drive, and the will to give it a shot.

> **Nothing about that point in my life was conducive to dropping everything and launching a career in bike racing. However, that's exactly what I did.**

This book captures the key lessons of my journey from cycling as a hobby to racing on a professional cycling team. The principles can be applied to anyone who has a dream and is willing to take a risk and spend time on the wrong side of comfortable. By reading this book filled with stories of characters, emotions, obstacles and successes, I hope you are inspired to take a step back and ask yourself if you are living your life to your fullest potential.

Through heart-wrenching low points and euphoric high points, I would never take back my short career as a professional cyclist. Through the process of dramatically morphing my career, lifestyle, routine, and physique, I learned life lessons on trade-off, boundaries, adaptability, moderation, relationships, integrity and the power of belief. I spent three years with incredible teammates from different countries and upbringings, of different ages and skillsets. The tools I gathered from these relationships and experiences are applicable to much more than cycling. These are principles that I use in my career, relationships, and day-to-day life.

It's never too late to be what you might have been.
—George Elliot

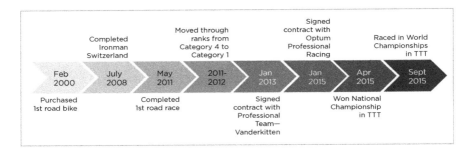

MENTAL STATE: *I am uncomfortable regarding the uncertainty of my future, but I've got to give it a try.*

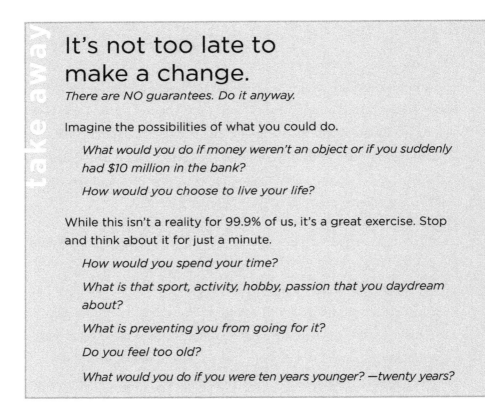

take away

It's not too late to make a change.
There are NO guarantees. Do it anyway.

Imagine the possibilities of what you could do.

What would you do if money weren't an object or if you suddenly had $10 million in the bank?

How would you choose to live your life?

While this isn't a reality for 99.9% of us, it's a great exercise. Stop and think about it for just a minute.

How would you spend your time?

What is that sport, activity, hobby, passion that you daydream about?

What is preventing you from going for it?

Do you feel too old?

What would you do if you were ten years younger? —twenty years?

Keep in mind that today is the youngest you will ever be, for the rest of your life! Unqualified? Too busy at work? What would you attempt if you were guaranteed not to fail? Fear of failure is what stops most people from following their passions. Most of us worry about attempting something and not being as good as we thought we were, looking stupid, losing money, disappointing loved ones, wasting time, or disappointing ourselves.

Do you find yourself asking questions about career choices that you have made? Is there a part of you that wishes that you had taken a different path? "Why didn't I get my MBA when I was younger?" "Why didn't I go to apply for a job at Facebook in the early 2000s?" "Why did I choose a career in X industry?" Do you feel like you're just going through the motions of your nine-to-five job? My response to you is that it is never too late to chase your dreams.

> **My response to you is that it is never too late to chase your dreams.**

Are you maximizing your performance in the areas of your life that matter to you? How would you measure the quality of your relationships, the fulfillment of your job or vocation, and your physical and mental health? Are you the best version of yourself that you can possibly be or do you feel like life is passing you by?

The tug to take a different path in your life or to take a risk is purely emotional. The reasons for not taking action are often driven by the rational decision-making process. Somewhere in the middle of the heart-versus-head debate lies the decision that allows you to take a calculated risk that will lead to an incredibly fulfilling outcome.

You may feel that life is starting to pass you by. You've reached your quarter life or midlife and don't feel that your life is as enriching as you once hoped or thought it would be. Perhaps you spent your twenties focused on your career and now you wonder what's next. Think through how you want to live the next several decades. In five years, what do you hope to have accomplished? Perhaps you feel that your friendships or relationships aren't as meaningful as they were in high school or college.

If you feel like you're simply going through the motions and not living your life to the fullest, this is something that you can change.

Before you quit your job and then wonder how you're going to make ends meet, I implore you to think through exactly what your interests are and what your passion is. What is it that occupies your mind? What is your absolute favorite activity? It might just be a simple shift from what you are doing now. It might be a major change. Start by taking small steps today, and put a plan around what the timing might look like. What trade-offs need to occur for you to make small changes?

The Wrong Side of Comfortable is intended to guide you through identifying what it is that inspires you, consider what it will take to get there, think through the critical steps to making it happen, and ultimately find the gumption to take the plunge. It is never too late to pursue an alternate career path, change your fitness habits, learn a second language, go to culinary school, play the guitar, take an accounting or graphic design course. It is never too late to develop your interest and take it to a new level.

CHAPTER THREE

Crossing the Line of "Normal"

*What I did not realize at that moment
was my life as I knew it would change
from that point forward.*

Discovering Passion

It took more than ten years from owning my first road bike
to competing in my first bike race, and I wouldn't change my
journey. Unlike any other sport, cycling is the one discipline
that came naturally to me. Although a dedicated swimmer in
high school, swimming 6,000-8,000 meters a day, I was smack-
dab in the middle of the pack in my best events. As a runner, I
dedicated myself to track workouts, endurance runs with proper
runners, and found myself slightly better than average in any given
running race. I had just completed an Ironman and did well in my
age group, but my time was not competitive with the professional
triathletes. On the bike, however, everything came to me more easily
than all of the previous sports in which I had participated.

Cycling is classed as a power sport. Unlike running, one could feasibly apply colossal amounts of torque to the pedals without the risk of injury. Whereas technique is everything in swimming, cycling requires a consistent, fluid rhythm where one can efficiently transfer her strength to forward propulsion. The French capture this "perfect" cyclist in a word: *souplesse*. This loaded word captures the harmony of the perfect pedal stroke that is gracefully powerful, combined with the dichotomy of the fluidity and intensity of the cyclist who is comfortably relaxed in the tight, streamlined, aero position.

Cycling is classed as a power sport.

At the age of twenty-three, the word *souplesse* was not on my radar. At the time, I might have struggled to distinguish between a road bike and a mountain bike, let alone what a proper cyclist looked like. With minimal understanding of the sport of cycling, my friend and colleague Kristin used gentle peer pressure to convince me to sign up for an Olympic distance triathlon. I agreed to join her in the St. Anthony's Triathlon. I knew that I would need to train for the race. Now I needed a bike. With exactly zero research about road bikes, I made my way to the closest bike shop to make the biggest (and best!) financial investment of my early twenties.

What I lacked in road bike knowledge, I made up for in enthusiasm for a new purchase. Testing a few bikes in the parking lot, I commented on how incredibly uncomfortable the saddles were. *Why do they make these saddles like tiny bricks,* I asked the salesman, with genuine curiosity. (Little did I know how much I would grow to appreciate a minimalist hard saddle.)

My other immediate concern and top priority was avoiding a humiliating crash in the parking lot as I attempted to balance on the incredibly skinny tires. Amused with my timid parking lot laps, the salesman assured me that it would be second nature in no time. Suspicious of his optimism,

I managed to keep the lightweight, foreign object in an upright position and avoided cycling trauma (at least on Day 1).

I liked the color of the bike, the fit seemed okay and I successfully rode in the parking lot without crashing. The salesman jested that I had selected a Rolls Royce due to the Campagnolo Record groupset. At the time, I had no idea if Campagnolo components were any good. Quite frankly, I didn't know what bike components were. Leaving the bike shop as the proud owner of my very first road bike, I had three immediate thoughts:

1. I had just spent the bulk of my savings with a $2,000 purchase.

2. I needed to track down a squishy saddle.

3. I had everything I needed to compete in a triathlon.

What I did not realize at that moment was my life as I knew it would change from that point forward.

I took my green Cannondale home and immediately ventured out on the flat, smooth roads around my neighborhood in

> Cycling became my social outlet, my meditation, my commuting method, my calorie burner, my stress reducer, my boyfriend/husband introducer and my travel catalyst.

Tampa, FL. With the first taste of the freedom that cycling offers, I headed straight out for twenty miles before I even considered turning around for my ride back home. In that two-plus hour journey, I experienced familiar roads with an entirely different perspective. I knew that I had found my sport.

Within the first three months of owning a road bike, not only did I compete in the St. Anthony's Triathlon, but I also participated in the ride across Florida, and a handful of other Century Rides (i.e., 100 mile rides) across the state. I was absolutely hooked on cycling! That said, it would take more than a decade from that first bike purchase for me to actually sign up for a bike race.

For the next fifteen years, cycling became one of the most meaningful and impactful aspects of my life. Cycling became my social outlet, my meditation, my commuting method, my calorie burner, my stress reducer, my boyfriend/husband introducer and my travel catalyst. My twenties can be summarized as working at a demanding corporate job in the financial industry that took me from Richmond, to Tampa, to DC, to Nottingham, England, to Steamboat, CO. The one constant that I had was my bike, and my passion for cycling. My closest friends and the most interesting locations that I ventured were a direct result of my passion for cycling.

HOBBY ———⟶ PASSION

Two events in my twenties revealed a pivot in that I could no longer refer to cycling as a hobby, but rather as a passion. Arguably, I crossed over the line of what is considered "normal." In these two experiences, I discovered my strength as a cyclist was the ability to ride for a very, very, very long time. Unnaturally, I would start to feel good after 50 miles and would come into my own around the 70-mile marker. I took immense pleasure in reporting to my cycling buddies that I was starting to feel "warmed up" once we were three hours into a ride. My soul-crushing comments usually allowed me to pull away from the group with a cheeky smile on my face, and their defeated sighs and head shakes.

Going-Away Present

The first event occurred when I was offered a job to work in Nottingham, England. I lived and worked in Washington, DC at the time and had a close group of cycling buddies whom I spent weekends with pedaling through hundreds of miles of Maryland, DC, and Virginia countryside. I told my friend Kyle that I wanted my going-away gift to be an epic ride the weekend before I was scheduled to leave town. We were accustomed to centuries and five to seven hours in the saddle, so Kyle knew that by *epic*, I meant business!

Kyle went to work with cycling maps and planned out a ride from his house in Georgetown in Washington, DC to Deep Creek, MD. The ride was 182 miles with 15,300 feet of climbing. It sounded absolutely perfect to me!

Rolling out on the eerily quiet roads of Georgetown at 5 a.m., we wouldn't arrive in Deep Creek, MD until 8 p.m., with a few fleeting moments of sunlight. We had just enough time to jump in the lake before heading out to replenish our calories. We gave

> **I started to understand the wrong side of comfortable.**

it our best effort with an extra-large pizza for an appetizer, followed by massive amounts of pasta for our main course and large brownie sundaes for dessert. Not only had I crossed the line of normal, I had a renewed sense of resilience and confidence, and a deep internal satisfaction of accomplishment. It is an incredible feeling to tap into endorphins and recognize one's strength.

How Are Your Thighs Going to Fit in Women's Jeans?

The second event that opened my eyes to cycling as my passion, and endurance as my strength, was when three friends and I decided to ride the entire Tour de France route in 2007. We planned the 2,130-mile route which would take a total of twenty-one days of riding with two rest days off the bike. These consecutive days of riding centuries certainly laid the groundwork for muscle memory, cycling stamina, and increased power. Three weeks living in a campervan, enduring days of eight hours in the saddle with rain pelting down, also demonstrated the challenging side of passion.

That particular year was an unusually wet one in France. The trying weather altered my image of blissfully riding through sunflower fields, eating warm baguettes from the Boulangeries, and enjoying stops in cafes in every small French village.

Many hours, and many miles of the journey around France were tough, to say the least. Those three weeks taught me the sweet spot that one discovers on the edge of suffering and accomplishing something meaningful. I started to understand the wrong side of comfortable. The fact that I even had the opportunity to take time off of work, travel around France, ride my bike and spend time with my friends was a luxury that was not lost on me.

> **Amy, what are you going to do with those legs? Do you think you'll even fit in women's jeans anymore? You can't waste them now.**

The four of us did complete the entire journey of the 2007 Tour de France course, EFI (Every *Flippin'* Inch) as we liked to report as our goal, our commitment, our mantra.

With tens of thousands of miles in my legs, combined with some decent athletic genetics, I knew I was a strong cyclist. Sitting on the steps of Champs Élysées, my dear friend Kyle Yost asked: *Amy, what are you going to do with those legs? Do you think you'll even fit in women's jeans anymore? You can't waste them now.*

In his distinct and direct style, he was challenging me to take my recreational riding to the next level. It would be an additional four years after that conversation that I finally competed in my first bike race.

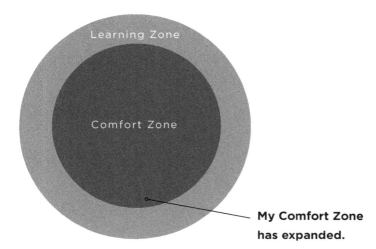

My Comfort Zone
has expanded.

MENTAL STATE: *I have expanded my comfort zone and I am starting to enjoy myself.*

A seemingly innocuous action may lead to a fundamental shift.

Sometimes the biggest life changes occur with a very simple step away from your routine. The response to the common struggle of "too much on our plates" is often, "you should learn how to say no." I suggest that you learn how to say yes to new experiences and to activities that will take you out of your comfort zone.

If you're struggling to identify your passion—let alone your interests and hobbies outside of family and work—you're not alone. Reflect on what you were doing ten years ago that you loved.

- Were you in high school or college?
- Besides drinking beer and hanging out with members of the opposite sex, what gave you fulfillment? What did you discover about yourself?

- What were you doing twenty years ago that you loved?

- What were your talents?

- Are those activities still options?

The best way to rediscover what gets you excited is to get out there and try something new: sign up for dance lessons; join a writing group; plan a trip to an unknown destination; join a gardening club; sample a new food or restaurant; call an acquaintance that you want to get to know better and meet her for coffee; sign up for a running race. The options to discover new areas of interest are endless.

These micro-detours from your routine may lead to hobbies that you love or even life-changing passions. Get out there and try something new!

CHAPTER FOUR

What Gives You Goosebumps?

*Your stress is when you're looking back
at what you did or didn't do.
Your anxiety is your fear of the future.
Your passion will put you in the moment.*

Cycling, My Nirvana

Cycling is undoubtedly my passion, from the very practical and literal experiential level of health, fitness, and speed, to the intangible level of focus, freedom, and clarity. I love the feeling of riding a bike, any bike. It starts with the routine of gathering the clothes and gear that I will need for the ride. It's picking the jersey, bib shorts, socks, helmet, sunglasses, gloves. It's applying lotion, sunscreen, lip balm, chamois cream, and pulling my hair into a ponytail that is the perfect height to slide under my helmet. It's starting the Garmin, as I throw my leg over the back wheel and clip into the pedals effortlessly.

A bicycle ride is a flight from sadness.

I feel the wind touching my skin as I take the first few pedal strokes. It's seeing the seconds ticking by as I slowly shift into an easy gear and pedal through the first few cycles. It's the initial feeling of pedaling squares, with a slight ache in my quads as the blood begins to pump through my muscles. It's the subtle transition to the rhythmic circles of smoothness and efficiency. It's the feeling of shifting into a bigger gear, the hum of the tires, strength in my legs applying power to the pedals, and watching my watts increase on the bike computer. It's feeling my heart rate escalate, hearing the sound of my breath, sensations of energy in my lungs, my legs, and my arms.

Cycling allows the purity of breathing and focus that can be compared to a meditative yoga class.

The speed of a bike ride is perfect for taking in the scenery. The average 18-22 miles per hour is not too fast or too slow. I am moving at just the right pace to view an ever-changing landscape, with the ability to take in the smells and sounds.

It's the internal negotiation with my legs and my mind on how much faster and longer I can/should/want to pedal. It's the journey of highs and lows during a ride. The rush I feel on a winding descent; the relief I feel with the gentle push of a tailwind. It's the tug of turning around to go home and relax the pressure on the pedals, followed by the drive to keep going and see if just for a moment, I can increase my cadence, and feel the satisfaction of the increased speed. I crave the rush that I feel, even on a training ride, when the pace picks up and the guys on the ride are feeling good.

As the pace soars, I'm fighting the desperate urge to slow down, not wanting to lose the wheel in front of me. It's that metallic taste in my mouth (blood, I assume), knowing that I'm hitting my limit. My mind has only one focus, and that is to stay on the wheel in front of me. Cycling is meditative and cathartic, and one of the only times in my life that I can genuinely say that I am thinking of nothing else. I am in the zone.

It's the feeling, after three hours in the saddle, of seeing the last mile up Fish Creek Falls Road, and eventually of taking the last turn onto my street, and the driveway. It's squeezing the brakes for the last time as my front wheel is one inch from the front door, the brake pads closing in on the rims, the bike coming to a complete stop. I clip out of my pedals, slowly, with more effort than when I started the ride. I lift my heavy leg over the saddle, walk my bike into the garage, plop myself down onto the bench, squeeze the sweat out of my helmet, unclick the strap of my helmet, and sigh, absorbing all of the energy running through my body.

It is then the critical moment of prioritizing basic human needs after a long ride: food, shower, sleep. Truth be told, I have stood in the shower with a sandwich in my hand, wondering how I will have the energy to complete the daunting 20-foot walk to my bed.

It's the "track-hack," the subtle cough that I have after a hard effort that can last up to three hours after I finish a ride. As all of the suffering ends when I stop pedaling, I find satisfaction with each cough, knowing that I put my body to the limit of its capabilities.

In addition to the physical pleasures of cycling, I love the escape that the bike offers. Cycling allows the purity of breathing and focus that can be compared to a meditative yoga class. There is a freedom and simplicity in cycling.

A bike ride fixes everything.

Through the simple act of applying pressure to the pedals, I take myself from one town to the next, covering sixty miles of road or dirt. That three-hour journey is mine, alone, to experience the range of pleasure and pain to the degree that my mind will allow on that particular day. As the miles tick by, nagging thoughts of life stresses percolate through my mind but escape with the increased intensity of my efforts, leaving me calm, grounded, and centered at the end of the ride. A bike ride fixes everything.

A sensation that takes one to that physical, emotional, even spiritual state is what I call passion. This feeling that I get from a challenging ride, where I am sufficiently out of my comfort zone, is how I define goosebumps.

Learning Zone

Comfort Zone

Reach for the stars.

Love what you do. Love what you do passionately. Find that thing that grabs you. Find the "why" that drives you.

> *What are you doing when you forget about time?*
>
> *What are you doing when you're not thinking about what you'll have for dinner or what is on your to-do list?*
>
> *What do you keep coming back to, year after year? This "activity" can be anything.*

You define it for yourself. Is it a sport, an instrument, dogs, travel, cooking, or writing? Think back to that talent that someone pointed out to you when you were fifteen years old. Wow, you have a talent for music. Have you considered learning to play the guitar? You are so good with animals; I can see you going to vet school. What is it that can occupy your mind so comprehensively that time stands still? Is it influencing teams, coaching, or pitching ideas?

DEFINE YOUR PASSION. What gives you goosebumps? Is there something that you are so passionate about that you forget about food, work, stress, money, comfort, and you live completely in the moment? Your stress is when you're looking back at what you did or didn't do. Your anxiety is your fear of the future. Your passion will put you in the moment.

Discover—or rediscover—what it is that drives you. You do this by getting outside of your comfort zone. The routine that you are tied to may be holding you back. What can you do that releases you from this hold and allows you to open the door to new opportunities?

take away

MENTAL STATE: *I have discovered what I love. I am driven to continue to push the limits.*

> **Don't ask yourself what the world needs;**
> **ask yourself what makes you come alive.**
> **And then go and do that.**
> **Because what the world needs is**
> **people who have come alive.**
> — Howard Thurman

PART II

Simple Actions, Extraordinary Results

CHAPTER FIVE

Tipping Point

Rise to the Top

I was all alone and in the front of the race,
and crossed the finish line first.
I didn't dare raise an arm in celebration.

In my case, it all happened quickly. I competed in my very first bike race, which was a hill climb up Lookout Mountain in Golden, Colorado, at the age of thirty-four. Although I had ridden a bike for a decade at that point, I had not made the transition from a mileage junkie to a racing cyclist.

A last-minute request and a dosing of peer pressure from a friend, I signed up for my very first bike race in Golden. Escaping the inevitable May winter storm in Steamboat, Kristen and I braved the treacherous drive over Rabbit Ears Pass through a blizzard. We arrived just minutes before the start of our race. She was literally pinning the race number on my back when the gun went off. We were both racing in the lowest amateur category of bike racing (i.e., Category 4). There were approximately thirty women in our race.

Propelled by adrenaline and perhaps some beginner's luck, I followed the wheels of the eight women who pulled away from the rest of the pack. Breathing heavily, but still controlled, I decided to ride around the woman in the front. To my utter shock, I started to pull away from her.

> **Fears aside, I won the race, and this result set the proverbial wheels in motion.**

And surprisingly, none of the other eight riders came with me. I was all alone and in the front of the race, and crossed the finish line first. I didn't dare raise an arm in celebration. I irrationally feared another rider passing me on the finish line. More rationally, I feared crashing myself out of the race with my substandard one-handed cycling skills. Fears aside, I won the race, and this result set the proverbial wheels in motion.

I spent the rest of the summer fully committed to learning about bike racing, racing categories, and types of races (time trials, road races, hill climbs, criteriums). I learned that I was a Category 4 racer until I competed in enough races, with top results, to earn sufficient points to become a Category 3 racer. At that point, I would race against a more competitive field and would need to win races to move up to become a Category 2 racer. The final amateur category in cycling is Category 1, and the next step is to become a professional cyclist by signing a contract with a Professional (UCI) racing team. The majority of cyclists stop at the Category 1 level, as there are only a handful of UCI teams in the US. They are highly selective, competitive, and can be political to join.

Over the course of the summer, I became maniacally focused on training, competing in races and winning races to move through the cycling ranks. I had a taste of the undeniable endorphins from each win, and I knew that I wanted to continue on that euphoric ride. By the end of the following summer, I had risen through the ranks from a Category 4 amateur cyclist to a Category 1 cyclist.

I sent my resume to every Elite and Professional cycling team in the US and eventually (after many rejections—see chapter on *The Art of Perseverance*) got a spot to race for the Vanderkitten Professional racing team.

Crossroads

My boss, also a cyclist, witnessed the progression from the sidelines with mixed feelings. I ecstatically showed him the upcoming race calendar with giddy enthusiasm of the famous races that I would compete over the upcoming months. Every couple of weeks there were races somewhere in the US in which my new racing team would be participating. My boss listened and his demeanor

> **It was time for me to make a decision: did I wanted to be a professional bike racer or did I want to manage Investor Relations at a billion-dollar hedge fund?**

changed from supportive cyclist to realistic boss. I was eventually called into his office to have the very challenging conversation of the "crossroads" that we had reached.

Bottom line, I had spread myself too thin and had reached the point that I could no longer do both. At the age of thirty-six, the more prudent decision might have been to stay with my job. It was a "dream" job in every sense of the word, i.e., a top-paying salary, located in Steamboat Springs, intelligent colleagues, advocates of work-life balance, interesting clients, enjoyable work.

> **To my boss, parents, colleagues, and many friends' disbelief, I opted for choice B ... to become a professional racing cyclist.**

Despite all of the incredible attributes of my job, I knew that I would look back at some point and wonder what might have been if I had really taken the leap and pursued professional racing. At the time, I even had the Olympics in the back of my mind. I knew that I was strong enough to at least be on a long list. To my boss, parents, colleagues, and many friends' disbelief, I opted for choice B ... to become a professional racing cyclist.

Got Money?!

The number one obstacle that I hear from friends, colleagues, and anyone who has considered making a major change is that they could not financially support that type of reckless career abandon. To be clear, I had not won the lottery, my husband made a very modest income, I was not a trust funder, and I did not make enough at the hedge fund to retire in my thirties. I recognized that I would have to make cuts in every area imaginable and creatively generate any income that I could muster to make my cycling career work.

The cuts that I made were endless. They included a zero-shopping policy for all unessential items (that many women may have considered essential items!) including clothes, shoes, lotions, makeup, nice shampoos, books. I did not subscribe to any memberships, such as Netflix, Spotify or SiriusXM. I did not eat meals out—ever. I used coupons at the grocery store and removed luxury items from my shopping cart such as organic vegetables, kombucha, and chicken that wasn't on sale. I limited my haircuts, eliminated pedicures, facials, and all other luxury treatments. Clearly, all first world sacrifices, nonetheless, I embraced a minimalist lifestyle.

On the income side, I coached a handful of athletes, taught spinning classes, and coached the Steamboat Triathlon Club whenever I was in town. My second year of racing, I found a part-time, location-neutral job to supplement my minimal cycling income. Through timing, luck, and perhaps a bit of karma, I found a job at a venture capital firm out of Boulder.

The firm was looking for someone with a corporate financial background similar to mine to do some administrative work, produce reports, newsletters, and manage their CRM. This was something that I could do from anywhere. I knew that I could easily find twenty hours during a week to work, but had to negotiate exactly when those hours would be.

> **I recognized that I would have to make cuts in every area imaginable and creatively generate any income that I could muster to make my cycling career work.**

There were times that I was fully absorbed in a stage race in Europe and couldn't even get my brain to type in a password, let alone generate a report. Conversely, there were times that I was up to my eyeballs in cycling news, stories, and thoughts, so I welcomed the distraction of the financial world. The work actually offered a welcomed outlet from bike racing. It also bridged the gap to help cover the mortgage.

My husband continued to work in Steamboat Springs at a small independent Insurance Agency. In a perfect world, he would have traveled to cheer me on in races, but this option was not financially viable with my significantly reduced income. The trade-offs we made were material and necessary for me to chase my cycling dreams.

> **Twenty years from now you will be more disappointed by the things you didn't do than by the things you did do. So throw off the bowlines, sail away from the safe harbor. Catch the trade winds in your sails. Explore. Dream. Discover.**
> —Mark Twain

Courage

There is nothing comfortable or easy about leaving a career to focus on a passion. I was officially on the wrong side of comfortable, more than I ever had been in my life. The obvious trade-off is losing financial stability.

My salary and benefits were eliminated overnight. The security of knowing what the future may hold disappeared in a moment.

I had more sleepless nights during the fall of 2013 than I can remember. My future was a complete unknown. Although I had a racing contract, I didn't know when or where I would race. My first year of racing, my contract did not include a salary and I didn't know how much I would pay out of my pocket for travel. I knew that I'd earn some money through race primes, and that I'd be given a cycling kit and bike equipment, but I still had bills and a mortgage to pay. And I still had to feed myself (and my ever-growing need for caloric intake)!

In addition to the financial stress, I was married. Matt, a former bike racer himself, was incredibly supportive. That said, we both knew that spending the majority of time apart for the extent of my cycling career would put a strain on our relationship. Neither of us knew how much time I would spend away, or what the future implications would be.

My future was a complete unknown.

Marriage, we had learned in our five years together, could be challenging in the best of times. Embarking into unchartered territory, both of us understood that surviving a long-distance marriage would require a new level of commitment and compassion.

Finally, my entire friendship base and social network were located in Steamboat Springs. Mountain resort towns, where like-minded athletic, adventurous, outdoor-loving individuals gravitate, foster tight-knit bonds of friendship. Knowing that I would be leaving this community for an unknown amount of time was unsettling. The unknown: scary … and exciting!

> **Ordinary courage is about putting our vulnerability on the line. In today's world, that's pretty extraordinary.**
> — Brene Brown, *The Gifts of Imperfection*

Putting the Wheels in Motion

Having signed a contract for the 2014 season and having left my job, I was halfway into my new life and had to take the full leap. It was mid-October, and I realized that a Colorado mountain town that receives approximately 400 inches of snow in a six-month period would not be the ideal training ground for road racing preparation. Tucson is a hot bed for aspiring professional cyclists to try to "make it," so I decided that I needed to immerse myself in this road cycling culture.

I had met Lynda, a Vanderkitten VIP, in September during a charity ride called the Canary Challenge. She mentioned that if I ever wanted to stay with her in Tucson, Arizona, she had extra room. Little did she know that I would take her up on that offer, repeatedly throughout my cycling career, well into my retirement, and likely for the next several decades! I stayed with Lynda for a week over Thanksgiving to check out the area and explore housing options. At the end of that week, I realized the following:

1 Lynda was going to become a very close friend.

2 Her home was ideal for me to spend the winter.

3 Tucson was a dream location for winter cycling.

Ultimately concluding that Tucson is to cyclists what Hollywood is to actors, I packed up my Subaru Outback on New Year's Day 2014, said good-bye to my husband, Matt; our dog, Lucy; and all of my friends in Steamboat Springs and made the solo trek to Tucson. The fourteen-hour drive allowed for some serious life contemplation. What was I doing at the age of thirty-seven, leaving behind a comfortable and fulfilled life to follow a dream with an unclear outcome that only a teenager or one in her early twenties would consider? At that moment, I was filled with doubt … but hope, too.

Despite my fear of the unknown, sadness in what I was leaving behind, I realized that my desire to be a professional cyclist and see how far I could take my cycling career justified the trade-offs that I was making.

MENTAL STATE: *I am uncomfortable. I have just exchanged every known for an indeterminate number of unknowns. I am on the edge of the learning and panic zone.*

Panic Zone

Learning Zone

Comfort Zone

There will be trade-offs.

Change requires massive amounts of courage.

Making a drastic change in one's life, regardless of the passion or vision driving the change, can be daunting. There will be many challenges and trade-offs, and often doubts about whether you have done the right thing.

Start where you are. Use what you have. Do what you can.
—Arthur Ashe

A common obstacle that cannot be ignored is how you can financially support yourself while you pursue your passion. This can be a tricky balancing act, and one that is unique to each individual. There are many ways to approach the issue. One option is to continue with your job and set a target for what milestone must occur to make a pivot feasible.

- Is there a certain amount of money that you must save first?

- Is there a date that makes sense to make the change?

- Are there clear results that you can achieve in what you're moving toward?

As an example, suppose you work in the corporate world and have a lucrative job with benefits. However, your interest and passion reside in the nonprofit sector. Recognizing that the nonprofit path will not fulfill your current financial demands, there may be options to fulfill your dream and not lose your home.

Brainstorm the financial cuts that you might be able to make in your life that will allow you to save money. Simultaneously, you can volunteer at a nonprofit to start

> **Having the courage to live on the wrong side of comfortable is a necessary step in accomplishing your goals.**

to get a sense of what the options are in that industry. You will need to think through the time cuts that you will need to make time for this extra activity. Perhaps your job, your significant other, and your fitness are your top three priorities. Could you sacrifice TV at night and spend that time on nonprofit work? Could you commute to work by bike and save money on gas and eliminate the need to go to the gym? Be creative. What are the small steps that you can start to make toward your goal?

If you have the will, you can accomplish your goal. You have to start somewhere, and you have to start sometime. Since we can't go back in time, you have to start now! Initiating the change will not get easier. You will never be 100% prepared. Having the courage to make the initial step, despite feelings of discom-

> **Define what you need to accomplish to take the full plunge.**

fort, is necessary. Anxiety and fear of failure are completely normal when taking a risk or heading toward the unknown. The initial step requires courage. Know that you will have hours, days, weeks, or even months that will be uncomfortable. Know that these feelings are part of the process in striving for and achieving your goals. Give it a go. Jump off the deep end head first. Having the courage to live on the wrong side of comfortable is a necessary step in accomplishing your goals.

CHAPTER SIX

Domestique
(Reality Check 1)

Uh-Oh, Do I Belong Here?

*It didn't take long for me to recognize
that the other riders had skills and
experience that I did not have.*

With enough miles in my legs and experience with other roadies, I was confident that I was a strong cyclist. However, I had risen through the cycling ranks fairly quickly and bike racing is very different from being a strong cyclist. From two summers of advancing through the amateur racing field, I knew that I was in the top five percent of cycling strength among women. The other side of the equation, which is equally if not more important, is positioning, tactics, general bike skills, and timing. These racing skills take years to acquire and perfect. With the bulk of my racing among smaller fields in Colorado, I had my work cut out for me in professional racing with fields of 100-plus racers. Having spent three years as the whale in the pond, my new life as a tadpole in the ocean was terrifying.

On my first professional team, Vanderkitten, it didn't take long for me to recognize that the other riders had skills and experience that I did not have. On our first day of camp, my team director handed me a suitcase with my name on it filled with a new cycling kit—shoes, helmets, sunglasses, chamois cream, and every other item that one needs to ride. We walked outside to see my sparkling new Wilier road bike. Receiving all of these items was beyond my wildest dreams.

We made a few adjustments to the saddle height and then ventured out on a fifty-mile team ride around the classic Mountain View roads. As incredible as it was to have all new equipment, it is not ideal to hop on a new bike, with new components, in a group that you've never ridden with, for a long ride. It can be a recipe for disaster. Fulfilling my biggest fear, I was left by my new teammates on the winding, technical descent. My teammates were all in front of me, and the team director was in a car, just behind me. I explained at the bottom that I was still getting used to everything, which was true. It was also true that I did not have the same technical skills that my teammates had. I was mortified to be the weakest link on the descent.

I was mortified to be the weakest link on the descent.

The next day, I did not fare much better. We were practicing motor pacing, i.e., riding one to two inches from the bumper of a car at 30 plus mph to simulate the leg speed and feel of riding in the peloton at full speed. I had never been that close to a bumper on my bike and was terrified. My mind raced through all of the 'what ifs' imaginable.

What *IF* the car hits a pothole?

What *IF* the car has to swerve?

What *IF* I hit a rock that I don't see?

What *IF* I tap the bumper and crash?

While all rational thoughts, this is not what one should be thinking traveling at 30 plus mph, or when one is attempting to be considered a professional racing cyclist. Incidentally, this would be nowhere near the highest speed or most dangerous motor pacing that I would do throughout my cycling career (see chapter on *Grit*). My teammates appeared to be calm, focused, and relaxed throughout our motor pacing sessions.

The first team camp was an indicator of some of the challenges that I would face in bike racing. It took everything I had to shut out the fear of crashing, accidents, and mishaps, and not let it get in the way of moving through the peloton, or launching a sprint. Even after three years of racing professionally in pelotons up to 200 women, on the narrow and cobbled roads of Europe, I never became fully comfortable with the risk of touching elbows at high speeds in large groups. Perhaps it was my age, the fact that I started racing late in life, or just my personality. I constantly had to work on improving my weaknesses and overcoming my fears.

> **I constantly had to work on improving my weaknesses and overcoming my fears.**

At this point, cycling was my career, and in order to succeed, I would have to make improvements. Three times per week, I found a large parking lot where I could practice skills such as unweighting my front and back wheels, picking up water bottles and flying around poles, light posts or cones at high speeds. I watched bike racing incessantly. I raced criteriums locally with men, and I even went to a hypnotist. I did everything in my power to work on overcoming my cycling fears through watching others, practice, and understanding the root cause of the issue.

One day, I overheard my team director tell a teammate that I was from a mountain town where the only traffic I encountered was moose, elk, and bears, so it was no wonder that I struggled in the peloton. My teammate responded that I was a "shotgunner," i.e., I was either at the front or in the back of the peloton—never in the group. The director had a point. Steamboat Springs certainly isn't Los Angeles, and I had literally run into the occasional wildlife on my rides! However, I knew that I didn't want that assessment to be my story. While working on my weaknesses, I figured out exactly what my strengths were and how I could best contribute to the team. Finding my niche within the pro field was critical to advancing my career, and finding success.

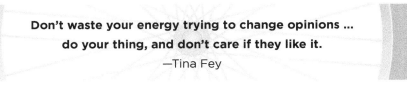

Don't waste your energy trying to change opinions ... do your thing, and don't care if they like it.
—Tina Fey

Domestique, Diesel Engine, Suffer Queen

I became the best domestique (i.e., team worker) that I could be. The domestique is the one who carries the water bottles, and one who sets up the sprinter/team leader for the last 200-400 meters. The domestique is the one who chases down the threatening attacks, or paces the team leader up a climb. If the team leader has a mechanical, the domestique stops with her, and gives her the bike if the team car is not immediately behind the group.

The job of domestique suited me perfectly. My focus was to protect my team leader and do everything in my power to save her for the final sprint. My personal final sprint would take place one to two miles before the finish line of the race. I would completely bury myself, knowing that my team leader was immediately on my wheel, and pedal until I literally couldn't move my legs any longer. Within a few hundred meters before the finish line, I would pull off the front, slow down my pedals, sit up from my tight and aero position, and the fate of the race would be in the hands (or legs!) or our team leader. Heaving and exhausted, I would crawl my way to the finish line as my teammate launched her sprint in the chaotic, high-speed dog fight to the finish line. My job was not to finish first. My job was to assist in having our team leader represented on the podium. The domestique exemplifies teamwork in assuming her role … defining the success of the larger group.

> My focus was to protect my team leader and do everything in my power to save her for the final sprint.

Another critical skill that I discovered in my second year of professional racing was the team time trial. The race consists of six riders who are in a perfect line, inches separating the wheel in front of them. It is an absolute maximum speed effort. The cyclist in front takes a pull as long as she can sustain, maintaining the pace and then drops to the back of the line without falling off the back of the group. It is an agonizing effort, regardless of how long. The controlled and focused nature of the race, combined with the sheer power, strength, and suffering required, was right in my wheelhouse. I had always been described as a diesel engine, and this is the exact skill that suits a time trialing team.

Optum Professional Cycling Team. Race simulation before World Championships: Annie Ewart, Maura Kinsella, Amy Charity, Jasmine Glaesser, Brianna Walle, Leah Kirchmann.

The third skill that I brought to the cycling team was my unwavering ability to suffer. My mom always told me that I had a high pain tolerance. This started when I burst an eardrum at the age of three. I quietly told my mom that I had an earache, and then stopped complaining for the next eight hours until she took me to see the family doctor, just to make sure it wasn't anything serious. This streak continued through all sports that I competed where coaches would sit me out due to my red face and how I appeared to be operating at or above my limits. I suffered a heat stroke during a triathlon that nearly killed me—hospitalized me for three days.

The ideal situation is when your passion aligns with your talent and skillset.

Bottom line, I had a history of having a stronger mind than body or at the very least, an incomprehensible ability to suffer. This characteristic is well suited for sport such as cycling, and became one of the characteristics that defined my racing.

In my third year of racing, I could describe my cycling strengths with clarity and confidence. I was a solid worker/domestique, a driving force on any time trial team, with an uncanny ability to suffer with the best of them. With these skillsets and characteristics on my resume, I landed a contract to race for Optum, one of the strongest racing teams in the US and world. Although my path to purchasing a race bike and launching a race career took thirty-four years, I discovered and defined my role to become a successful racing cyclist.

Panic Zone

Learning Zone

Comfort Zone

> **Do not let what you cannot do
> interfere with what you can do.**
> —John Wooden

MENTAL STATE: *I am on the edge of the Learning Zone and with periods crossing over into the Panic Zone. I am uncomfortable. Have I made the right choice?*

Focus on your strengths.

Define your story. Own your story.

The ideal situation is when your passion aligns with your talent and skillset. As a side note, in following your passion, we are operating under the assumption that this is something that you do relatively well. If you aspire to sing at the Grammys, but can't carry a tune, then you may want to reevaluate your goals. Assuming that you are not only talented, but find yourself to be better than most at what you are attempting, then you are on the right track.

Once you define your passion, vision and goals, it can be terrifying to take the initial step in pursuing your dream. When you start to think through the challenges ahead, you might be filled with negative thoughts. It's easy to question if you are actually ready to take on such a feat. You might start comparing yourself to others who have mastered your skill and conclude that they are younger, smarter, stronger, or generally more qualified. The key difference is that you are on your own journey. Everything

Know what it is you can do better than anyone else and do that.

in your life has happened to get you to this point. You may be starting later, or at a different stage, but do not discount all of the experience that you have gained in getting to that point.

There is room for all of us to find success within our own niche. Be precise about your area of expertise and don't worry about what others have done to get to a similar point. You are driving the path and it doesn't have to look like anyone else's.

Within your area of expertise, you will find elements where you excel and others that are more challenging for you. Focus on those areas that come more naturally to you. For example, if you are interested in music, and you don't have a great voice, and you are not especially talented on the guitar, you may want to focus on writing songs. Narrow your focus to your area of expertise and your talent. Do not focus the majority of your time on learning the guitar or taking voice lessons. Focus your time on writing music. You can apply this concept to any talent area. If you're trying to get your fitness back and you struggle to run more than ten feet, you can focus on exercise classes or hiking or cycling.

Relentlessly work on being the absolute best that you can be in the area where you are already strong.

Also, do not forget those traits that are inherent and do not even seem like they are specific skills. For example, are you nurturing? Do you have the ability to make others feel great through a few words? Are you the type of person who is constantly looking out for and taking care of others? Do you respond well in emergency situations? Are you the one who is able to remain calm when others are not? In addition to your skillset, think through the traits that will support the interest or passion that you will pursue. If these complement each other, you have found the ideal situation.

You do not need to master your weaknesses within your goal. Relentlessly work on being the absolute best that you can be in the area where you are already strong. You can spend an indefinite amount of time trying to improve your weaknesses. You will likely have some success, but the gains may be minimal. To become your best, think with razor-sharp focus of your passion and your defined skillset, and you can reach levels that you never thought possible. You are on your own journey. Everything in your life has happened to get you to this exact moment.

CHAPTER SEVEN

Dare to Dream

*I tried to imagine what it must feel like
to have all of the stars align
so that my timing, form, equipment,
and mental state all came together
for the win of a lifetime.*

I allowed myself to daydream about cycling, arguably to an unhealthy degree. I had a picture in my mind of a crowd six people deep, lining up along the last three miles of the road, Tour de France style. I was in a breakaway of six riders and I was the only one on Team USA in the break. With just over a mile to go, I could hear the roar of the crowd. I sat on the third wheel going into the final turn. I could see the signs above counting down the meters until the finish. My lungs were on fire, my legs burning; I was absolutely at my limit. My mind focused. Nothing mattered but getting across the finish line first. With 300 meters to go, I came around the two riders in front of me. I was out of the saddle, fighting with everything I had.

My husband was standing on the side of the road dramatically jumping up and down. "Bury yourself, Amy!" he screams. Finishing just centimeters in front of my competition (a well-known European racer), I threw my arms into the air. With sweat pouring down my face, I was overcome with exhaustion and euphoria.

I replayed this image in my mind time and time again. I went to sleep with this thought and allowed myself to dream what it would feel like.

Allow yourself to daydream. During endless miles of training rides, I would day-dream about throwing my arms up and hearing the deafening enthusiasm from the crowd.

I watched bike races on YouTube on a daily basis, and replayed the final sprint of each race to see the various methods that helped professional cyclists win races. I tried to imagine what it must feel like to have all of the stars align so that my timing, form, equipment, and mental state all came together for the win of a lifetime.

This particular vision is important in what it demonstrates.

1 It is ambitious.

2 It was on repeat in my mind.

3 It captures the "what" in detail, but without any restriction on the how I will get to that point in my cycling.

4 It is an image that captures my passion.

5 It causes goosebumps when I think about it.

> **Vision animates, inspires, transforms purpose into action.**
> —Warren Bennis

MENTAL STATE: *I'm allowing myself to dream without barriers or restraints.*

Clarify your vision.

Summon this image to the front of your mind.

Once you have identified your passion, allow yourself to visualize what your life would be like if you were to pursue that passion. Daydream about what it looks like, at its best, with you in your element. Explore the ideas with your friends. Let your imagination go wild. Truly embrace the idea of yourself in that particular job, career, setting that would be your ideal. Write it down. Put Post-it notes around your house. Save pictures and images of what it would look like. Create a Pinterest board and pin everything relating to this image. Join groups that have the same dream, vision, or passion. Get out and talk to people, and share your dream. Train your mind to visit that image repeatedly. Visit it often and with no barriers.

Allow yourself to daydream. Articulate your vision to your friends and your family. Be specific. How does it feel, smell, and taste? What are your sensations? It doesn't have to be a sporting competition. What does it look like?

CHAPTER EIGHT

It's Starting to Get Real

*I wanted to be
the best racing cyclist
that I could be.*

With my image of winning an International race in mind, I wrote down the key goals that would help me reach my vision. I am sharing the goals that I set and communicated with my coach prior to racing professionally. Recently looking back at what I had written, I found the progression interesting, in that certain goals took *years* to achieve. Other goals, seemingly audacious, I accomplished the year that I set them. Regardless of the timeline, the point is that I had something concrete that motivated me to train on the days that I did not feel like training. My coach had clear guidelines in what I hoped to achieve, and we were completely aligned on the direction I was heading. Finally, measuring my progress simply required me to review my goals and check off what had been done and what areas I still needed to tackle.

My Cycling Goals

Race with Category 1 & Category 2 women
(Goal 2011, Accomplished 2011)

Win CO State Road Race Championship
(Goal 2011, Accomplished 2011 & 2012)

Win CO State Hill Climb Championship
(Goal 2011, Accomplished 2011 & 2012)

Sign a contract with a top 10 UCI Racing Team
(Goal 2013, Accomplished 2015)

Race for the USA National Team
(Goal 2011, Accomplished 2014 & 2015)

Achieve a top 10 result in a NRC
(National Racing Calendar) race
(Goal 2013, Accomplished 2015)

Win a National Championship
(Goal 2013, Accomplished 2015)

Race in a World Championship
(Goal 2014, Accomplished 2015)

A goal is a dream with a deadline.
—Napoleon Hill

What Gets Measured Gets Done

I had to begin to measure and record my cycling data. I purchased a power meter to track my output and a Garmin bike computer to measure the distance, elevation, and specific interval laps. I created an account with Strava—a social media site where I could document my mileage and compare my times on specific segments to other cyclists. After completing each ride, I would upload my cycling files to review my power and performance and share it with my coach for analysis.

In my case, examples of continuous action were:

- Train 15–20 hours per week

- Achieve racing weight

- Limit physical activity outside of cycling (e.g., swimming, hiking, running)

- Limit or eliminate alcohol

- Spend two hours per week on bike skills and drills

Some actions are accomplished with one step. Examples include:

- Buy a power meter and track cycling data

- Hire a coach

- Contact the decision-maker for the National Team

- Reach out to professional teams

Lycra Clad, Shined Shoes, and Lean

I wanted to be the best racing cyclist that I could be. Some of the steps that I took were major life changes; however, the initial seemingly small steps were critical as well. For example, I started to understand how to "look the part" as a cyclist. I noticed that all racing professionals were immaculate in how they dressed. Even on training rides, their cycling kit was clean, fitted, and matching. Their bikes sparkled. Their socks were a minimum of four inches high. Their helmets, shoes, and sunglasses were shined.

Professional cyclists always seemed to wear a few more layers of clothing than amateur cyclists. If the temperature was 59 degrees, professional cyclists would wear leg warmers, arm warmers, and a vest. I adopted the 60-degree rule and added a few extra layers during my rides.

In addition to looking like a professional cyclist, I hired a coach to guide me through a proper training plan and to better interpret my cycling data. Up until that point, my training plan consisted of long rides whenever I could squeeze them in and fast rides whenever there happened to be a few Steamboat Springs guys available to join me. A coach and a training plan shifted these arbitrary miles to purposeful and intentional training objectives. I sought fast group rides that simulated racing speeds. Rather than riding alone and attempting to reach my max speed and power relying on just my own motivation, I put my legs to the test with cyclists who were stronger than me.

When you achieve your goals, celebrate them.

I'll never forget walking into work and reading the email from my coach Jeff. It was a "feedback sandwich" email. He communicated that he thought I. "displayed more potential than any athlete he had worked with..."

Jitters filled my belly as I continued to read. "However," (I braced myself for the constructive feedback) he communicated that "an area where I could benefit would be by a little weight loss over time."

He was incredibly diplomatic, polished and thoughtful in his messaging. Not to mention, absolutely correct in his assessment.

He suggested that I "look for some free ways to cut a small amount of calories every day and any shift towards lower calorie dense foods like veggies." He proposed ideas such as "portion management: smaller meat & starch portions, larger veggie portions. Smaller portions of desserts, or selection of desserts with fewer calories." He finished his email concluding that he thought that I would make it to the top level of the sport.

Admittedly a hard pill to swallow as I had always considered myself a healthy weight, I began to find areas where I could cut calories. I followed Jeff's recommendations and began to make subtle changes to my diet and dessert habits. The lighter one is, while maintaining the same level of power, the faster she will ride. This power-to-weight ratio is especially true on climbs.

Dressed like a professional cyclist, following a proper training plan and making headway on having a cyclist's physique, I knew I must also surround myself with cyclists. Early in my cycling career, my husband and I started the routine of driving from Steamboat Springs to Boulder, a three-hour drive, to do the Boulder group ride called the Gateway Ride. The snowy roads and the *ski powder or bust* mindset that permeated our little town prevented any hope of road rides or group rides in the winter. We planned our winter weekends around day trips with seven hours of total driving time for three hours of total riding time. Our entire social life and routine shifted with these weekend rides, but the trade-offs were important in order to take steps toward my ultimate cycling goals.

Although I was not a professional at that point, I made a concerted effort to move in that direction. I put it out there that I was serious about becoming a top racing cyclist.

MENTAL STATE:

I am consciously and proactively leaving my Comfort Zone and have both feet in the Learning Zone.

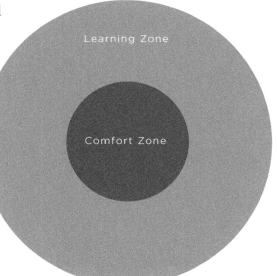

One key benefit of having goals is it can help you make decisions. For example, the decision of whether or not you should join your friends for happy hour after work can be evaluated against your short-term goals.

This decision may have no impact on your overall goals. The question of whether you should take your dog on a five-mile hike might be evaluated against your goals. Should you spend the weekend camping? You can consider each decision by evaluating it against your goals. You may begin to ask yourself, will this activity help or hurt my goal of following my dream?

Articulate your dream with specific goals.

Write it down! Make a plan. Look the part.

Once you are clear about your passion and you have a vision in mind, it is time to set goals. You might love setting goals and are intimately comfortable with SMART goals (Specific, Measurable, Attainable, Realistic and Time Based). For those of you who are anti-goals, I humbly implore you to consider them. They serve a purpose.

To have begun is to have done half the task ....
—Horace

Secondly, goals help you gauge if you are on track. It is easy to assess where you stand against what you had planned. Are you on track to save enough money to enroll in a class? If your goal is to set aside $500 per month, you can easily evaluate if you are in the right spot financially. Are you on track to run a 10-kilometer race in the summer? You can simply check in on your current mileage and have an objective response to this question.

Goals provide a framework and a sounding board to more easily make decisions and drive actions.

Goals allow you to remove some of the subjectivity and make a logical estimation of exactly where you stand.

Finally, goals allow you to reflect on your accomplishments. It's a great exercise to look back and see which goals you knocked out of the park, and which goals you still need to work toward. When you achieve your goals, celebrate them. It is common for goal setters to take their achievements for granted and move onto the next one, which may be more ambitious than the first.

Celebrating your achievements is a key element to how the goal setting process works. You set a goal, you realized that you have accomplished the goal, you celebrate your achievement (ideally, with others who are supportive of your goal), your adrenaline from success motivates you to start to tackle the next goal on your list, and the cycle repeats itself. Before you know it, you've knocked several goals out of the park. And the new goals—the ones you originally didn't think were possible—are now what you're striving for.

> **Define exactly what it is that you are striving for. Write it down.**

Pen to Paper

Identify what you want in life more than anything else. What brings you to life? What makes you feel like you are living life to the fullest? The dream could be traveling to a foreign country, dramatically changing your career, playing an instrument or participating in a 10-kilometer run. There are no boundaries.

Define exactly what it is that you are striving for. Write it down. What is your goal? Keep the goal in front of you as much as possible. Make copies and hang them around your house, in your car, as your screensaver. Create weekly notifications that are sent to your phone and your computer. Print out an image of what this goal looks like to you. Surround yourself by the image, words, and sounds of this goal.

Understand exactly what it is going to take for you to implement your goal. You must flush out each goal by writing the specific actions that lead to your accomplishing it. What are the continuous steps that you will take? What are the one-off actions that get you closer to where you are heading? Be methodical.

If your life dream is to spend an entire summer living in Italy, for example, start taking small steps that demonstrate that you are committed to getting there. Write down, "I will live in Italy in the summer of 2020." Find images of the Trevi Fountain, Cinque Terre, and the Leaning Tower of Pisa. Use these images as bookmarks, magnets, screensavers. Buy travel books on Italy and fiction books with Italian characters. Join clubs that discuss Italian culture. Enroll in a language class. Start a travel fund and add $5/day to the pot in lieu of your daily coffee. Assuming the bigger hurdle is getting time off of work, think through ways that you can make this happen. Can you plant the seed for a sabbatical in two years' time? Can you suggest an opportunity to work remotely? Could you train a colleague to handle some of your work? Can you find an English class to teach in Italy to help pay the bills? Be creative.

Think through and write down goals that are ambitious. These goals may take you months or even years to achieve. Once you have written down your goals, develop an action plan that will get you there. Pull out your Google calendar and plot a few dates. The first should be in a week, and then in a month, and in six months. What are the actions that you can take within the next seven days? What hurdle do you need to surpass to make even bigger changes that may occur in a month?

Start with a general timeline in Excel, Power Point or on a white board. Put a few major accomplishments by date. What do you hope to accomplish by the end of the month? Do you want to have increased your running mileage from three miles to five miles? Do you want to have raised a certain amount of money to enroll in a class? Put a stake in the ground. Look the part for what you want to accomplish. You will start to find supporters and like-minded individuals, and you will start to convince yourself that you are on the path to realizing your dreams.

PART III
Test Your Limits

CHAPTER NINE

Be a Monk

I had taken a major plunge in moving to Tucson.
Now what? I called my coach, Jeff, to discuss the
big picture. Jeff was a former professional cyclist, a
collegiate national champion, and had a law degree.
In short, he was intelligent, competent, experienced,
and I trusted him unconditionally. Jeff and I talked
about the 2014 race schedule that would include nine
days of racing in El Salvador in late February. I had seven
weeks to get as fit as possible. At that point, I had jumped
in the deep end, so it made sense to go all the way by doing
everything possible to be the best cyclist I was capable of
being. Jeff and I discussed nutrition—dessert and wine, my
weight, sleep, social life ... so basically all of the "norms" that
had created my life balance.

"When I was living and racing in Spain, I pretty much lived like a
monk. It's only seven weeks. See what happens," Jeff said to me.

I couldn't think of any reason not to try to live that lifestyle and see
what would happen, knowing full well that I would be out of "balance"
(i.e., everything in my focus would be cycling).

The Mantra: Live like a monk.

Jeff and I established a set of rules to eliminate any confusion as to what I should or should not do.

The Rules:

1 Six training days per week on the bike

2 One glass of wine the night before a rest day

3 Dessert one time per week

4 Naps after all long rides (i.e., rides that were > three hours)

5 Minimum of eight hours of sleep per night (not including nap)

6 Recovery drinks after all rides (excluding recovery/coffee ride)

7 One recovery ride per week

8 Minimal activity outside of cycling (including walking, swimming, standing, hiking)

9 Send cycling data and perceived health scores on a daily basis

There, I had it. The Rules to live by for seven weeks, because … well, why not? If I was giving the Professional Cycling career a shot, it made sense to really go for it. To be clear on the "perceived sacrifices," training six days per week is what I was already accustomed to, so I had absolutely no issue with committing to that lifestyle. I knew a forced daily nap was not going to be an issue either!

> In this time of redefining the "norm," my life changed dramatically.

The real heartache stemmed from limitations on wine, dessert, and general activity off the bike, not to mention seven weeks away from my husband, dog, friends and community of Steamboat Springs. By no means was I a big drinker, but I can certainly appreciate a glass of wine or two with a meal. A dessert restriction was in a different ballpark. I was accustomed to ten to fifteen desserts per week, if I counted the cookies after lunch and chocolate or ice cream after dinner. How was I going to go from fifteen to one? Now that was sacrifice!

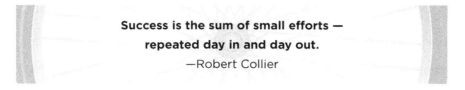

**Success is the sum of small efforts —
repeated day in and day out.**
—Robert Collier

In this time of redefining the "norm," my life changed dramatically. I reviewed my weekly training schedule with my coach, and found the appropriate group rides every day of the week, and we put together the schedule that I would follow.

The Schedule:

Monday – Rest day, no riding.

- *Riding Time*: N/A

- *Group*: N/A

- *Description*: Grocery shopping, laundry, errands, clean bike, read outside, call mom, dad, husband, sister.

Tuesday – Gates Pass/Tuesday Shootout (with two hour add-on)

- *Riding Time*: Three to four hours

- *Group*: Pro teams, Masters racers, retired pros, speedy women, etc.

- *Description*: Start at University for a short, fast-paced training ride that ends at the top of Gates Pass. The ride begins at a conversation pace as it leaves the busy streets of Tucson. The sound of friendly chatter is soon replaced with gasps for air, gear clicking, wind rushing, and occasional callouts of impending obstacles. Considering that the roads are choppy, bumpy, winding and contain potholes and sand sections, the pace is relentless.

- *Purpose*: Race simulation, high intensity, endurance
- *Memory*: I held on for dear life every Tuesday, and remembered to breathe again once I was at the top of Gates, regrouping, and getting ready to add on additional miles with the other Pro (unemployed, i.e., those of us that didn't have to rush off to work) cyclists.

Wednesday – Pistol Hill

- *Riding Time*: Three to four hours
- *Group*: DOGS (self-identified as Old Guys). Turns out, they're primarily men in their 40s, 50s, 60s, serial trainers, former racers.
- *Description*: Meet every Wednesday morning at the cycling mecca, Le Buzz, and set out on a two-plus hour tempo ride.
- *Purpose*: Tempo with minimal intensity, endurance
- *Memory*: The DOGS group might not look to be the fastest group in the parking lot, but don't be fooled … these guys tear it up on several of the sections and have many of the fast racers hanging on by a thread.

Thursday – Functional Threshold Power (FTP) Efforts

- *Riding Time*: Two to three hours
- *Group*: Solo
- *Description*: Various lung-busting intervals with a specified amount of rest between. Typically, on a flat and quiet road.
- *Purpose*: Increase FTP, power, strength, speed
- *Memory*: Isolation in the middle of the desert. Often had irrational concerns that I had unintentionally crossed over the Mexican border. (clearly my brain was not receiving enough oxygen during these efforts.)

Friday – Recovery Ride (aka Coffee Ride)

- *Riding Time*: 90 minutes

- *Group*: friends or solo

- *Description*: Little ring pedaling keeping watts below 130, no hills, conversation pace.

- *Purpose*: Spin legs with a high cadence, recovery.

- *Memory:* Exploring Tucson. Enjoying coffee with new friends.

Saturday – Shootout! *

- *Riding Time*: Five to six hours

- *Group*: the fast boys, i.e., Pro Men

- *Description*: Outrageously intense ride led by well-known professional male cyclists on top US racing teams, with the objective of tearing each other's legs off, so to speak.

- *Purpose*: High intensity, endurance, race simulation.

- *Memory*: Finding myself on the wheel of professional male cyclists that I watched on TV, wondering if I was still alive due to the fact that my heart rate was in the 190s.

Sunday – Mt. Lemmon

- *Riding Time*: Four to five hours

- *Group*: strong guys or solo

- *Description*: 25-mile climb with the elevation of 9,157 ft summit

- *Purpose*: Build strength and power. Simulate climbs in upcoming races.

- *Memory*: The Mt. Lemmon Cookie Cabin featuring a warm, straight-out-of-the-oven homemade cookie the size of my head. (Fortunate that our minds gravitate toward remembering the positive and shutting out many of the rough patches.)

A Weekly Dose of Uncomfortable

*The Saturday Shootout is the Tuesday Shootout on steroids (at the risk of using an inappropriate metaphor in a book about bike racing). The ride began with anywhere from 150-200 riders. My first Shootout, I walked out of the bathroom and straight into the back of a very pro-looking guy in Garmin kit, who turned out to be Tommy Danielson. I gave him a shy smile and realized that I could pretty much rule out the idea of a steady ride that day. In addition to having legitimate professionals swarming University Blvd moments before the ride, a Mavic wheel car appeared to follow the group ride (!), as well as Tommy D's personal follow car, and the occasional team car when continental professional teams were training in the area. To be clear, it was not normal to have follow cars on training rides.

The Saturday Shootout did not disappoint. After a lovely conversation pace for the initial four miles, the attacks began as soon as we passed the infamous Valencia Road.

With varying degrees of success in staying with the fast guys on the Shootout ride, I managed to put myself in the PAIN CAVE every single Saturday.

The Shootout ride, in particular, was as fast as any race in the female professional peloton. I treated the Shootout as a race day. The night before I set aside all of my cycling kit, ensured that my bike was clean and ready for the ride. I woke up two hours before I had to leave the house to ensure that I could eat and digest a sufficient amount of oatmeal to get me through the first few hours. I left Lynda's house with plenty of time to ensure that if I got a flat in route to the ride that I would have time to fix it.

Boredom never entered the equation on these five-hour rides. The intensity of the pace allowed my brain to auto-play three thoughts. Don't lose the wheel in front of you; drink and eat; and watch for attacks.

In summary, the Shootout continued to be uncomfortable and terrifying every single Saturday, and yet served as the best preparation imaginable for the upcoming race schedule.

Settle In

Operating under the strictness, yet simplicity of The Mantra, The Rules, and The Schedule, I settled into my Tucson routine without detour. There was something comforting about eliminating decisions and living the simple lifestyle prescribed by my coach. I relished my routine of eating a trough of oatmeal, riding, gulping down a chocolate and almond milk recovery drink, showering, eating lunch, washing cycling kit, napping, reading email and making calls, stretching, eating dinner with Lynda and Eric, sleeping. Repeat.

> I can confidently look back and take comfort in the fact that I gave it my all.

There were a few key factors that made it easy to embrace the sacrifice and conform to my life of monotony. The fact that I lived in Tucson among thousands of cyclists—hundreds of which were professional— I was surrounded by those striving for similar goals and living the same lifestyle. Had I stayed in Steamboat, there would have been pressure to go to Happy Hour, go out for dinner, and stay up later than planned, and of course, having other activities at my disposal, such as skiing, fat biking, hiking, swimming, and running. Surrounding myself by those with the same agenda as me removed most of the distraction that I might have otherwise had.

> Far and away the best prize that life offers
> is the chance to work hard at work worth doing.
> —Theodore Roosevelt

After the seven-week period, I was cycling fit. I had reached my "race weight." I was confident, and I was ready for the upcoming season on my first professional cycling team. Living a structured life in Tucson allowed me to test my limits. Over that seven-week period, I did everything that is considered recommended practice for aspiring cyclists. I can confidently look back and take comfort in the fact that I gave it my all.

MENTAL STATE:

I am unquestionably in the Learning Zone.

Remove distractions.

Find mastery in routine and monotony. Discover fulfillment in sacrifice.

Once you have progressed from having an idea to making a decision to pursue your passion, you will need to make immediate, and sometimes drastic, changes to your daily routine. Although it can be viewed as "sacrifice", you can find comfort in simplified choices that all lead you to accomplishing your goal. Deciding that you are willing to make the changes necessary to go after the improved version of you is the first and critical step. Having the idea and actually taking steps to work toward your goals are very different. The latter requires a level of commitment to getting where you want to be. Establishing a set of rules and routine to live by allows you to eliminate the guesswork.

Amy training in Tucson during "Monk" phase.

> Nothing in the world can take the place of persistence.
> Talent will not; nothing is more common than
> unsuccessful men with talent. Genius will not;
> unrewarded genius is almost a proverb.
> Education will not; the world is full of educated derelicts.
> Persistence and determination alone are omnipotent.
> —Calvin Coolidge

In order to pursue your dream, think through the trade-offs that are required of you. I try not to think of these choices as sacrifices. They are, in fact, choices. To the extent that is realistic in your situation, remove distractions. Write a set of rules that you will live by and make yourself accountable by relaying your progress to someone on a regular basis. This can be a coach, a friend, or a family member. Commit to your rules and process and follow this process religiously. Track down your progress and send updates with quantifiable data and context on how you are feeling mentally and physically.

I try not to think of these choices as sacrifices.

To make the rules more palatable, set a time limit that you will commit to following the rules. Surround yourself with people who are striving to do something similar (it can be online groups, forums, networking lunches, etc.). Establish trade-offs that allow you to test the parameters of what you are capable of.

CHAPTER TEN

Off Balance
(Reality Check 2)

"You Look Like a Little Fella."

In my cycling-obsessed bike racing mind,
I was just about where I needed to be.

My first year as a Professional Cyclist, I did not
have a job. I intentionally lived a life that was out
of balance. Cycling was everything to me. Reviewing my
Twitter, Instagram or Facebook feeds, one would conclude
that the only news in the world centered around bike racing.
I declined almost all activities that weren't directly related to
improving my chances of becoming a successful bike racer.
Almost every action in my life centered around understanding
cycling, improving myself as a cyclist, and researching bike racers.

My husband came out to visit me after my training stint in Tucson.
"Darling, you look like a little fella," he said to me in his British accent.

He observed my protruding cheekbones, my defined jaw, my concave belly,
my pelvic bones and ribs on display, my flattened chest, and my ripped
quad muscles. In my mind, his comment was the biggest compliment I

could have received. I officially had the body of a cyclist. Seven weeks of The Mantra, The Rules, and The Schedule had paid off.

The question that I started to ask myself was: *Why would I do anything that might hinder my dream of becoming the best cyclist possible?* The "why would you" line of thinking can lead down a slippery slope.

Why would you ever eat chocolate, or cheese, or pizza if you're asking your body to maximize output?

Why would you go to your cousin's wedding when you know that you'll be standing and dancing into the night? Getting to bed early, sitting and relaxing are undoubtedly better preparation for a training day.

Why would you go out to dinner with friends and potentially have limited healthy options? Clearly, a hearty salad is a better option for feeling healthy.

Why would you have a full-time job when competitors are training and recovering every day? The "cousin's wedding" question can translate into any decision that you're making.

Why would you go on a walk or hike with friends, why would you meet them out for happy hour when it isn't helping achieve your goal?

It turns out that I was so maniacally focused and obsessed with cycling and my performance, that I could not perform.

The first few races that I did after living in Tucson, I expected to be flying because I had done everything right and followed The Mantra, The Rules, and The Schedule.

I was twelve pounds lighter than my normal weight. I didn't have a menstrual cycle. My only news was related to bike racing. I declined every social event. I didn't see my friends or my husband for weeks or months at a time. In my cycling-obsessed bike racing mind, I was just about where I needed to be.

Have a Glass of Wine, FFS!

I met up with my former teammate, Jenn, for a ride in Boulder. I was in the middle of my season with Vanderkitten and ten days away from flying to Europe with the USA National Team to race in the Czech Republic, Belgium, and the Netherlands. After an hour climb, Jenn and I stopped at a coffee shop. She asked how I was doing mentally and if I was excited for Europe.

"Actually, my numbers are down. I don't have any snap in my legs," I responded. "I feel like I'm under-trained. Do you know how much the other girls ride? Twenty-plus hours per week. I'm not doing anything near that amount of time. I'm worried that I'll race poorly over there and never have another opportunity to race in Europe."

"Amy!" Jenn said, giving me her very serious face. "You are absolutely trained enough. If anything, you are borderline over-trained. You need a week off the bike. Promise me you will not look at your bike for the next seven days. Do not look at Twitter or Instagram or Facebook for the next seven days. Have a glass of wine, FFS! Eat dessert. Spend time with your husband. Have a normal person's week and you will be flying by the time you get to Europe."

Jenn, who appropriately prided herself on being my "alpha friend," had a decade of racing under her belt and could smell burnout from 100 miles away. I was so wrapped up in my own head that I didn't realize that I needed rest. It seemed inconceivable that taking a few days off would be helpful, when I thought that I actually needed more mileage. The idea of seven days without riding was incomprehensible at the time. That said, I listened to her advice and tried out life as a civilian (i.e., non-cyclist) for one week. I made an effort to spend time with friends, I reconnected with my husband, I read news and books unrelated to cycling, I shifted my focus from myself to those around me, and it was the best thing I could have done.

Jenn was absolutely right. I had my best results in Europe that summer with a podium in a UCI road race and fourth place in the GC. My pendulum had swung too far toward bike racing and I needed a good friend and a reminder that sometimes it's okay to take a pause and reset.

Many aspects of the routine and disciplined life were critical to my success. Furthermore, there was certainly great value in the time that I spent in Tucson living like a monk. That said, it became clear that some of the restrictions that I placed on myself were too severe for me to be healthy and successful. I discovered my personal boundaries.

> **For me, a few extra pounds, a few swims and hikes, social time with family and friends, a handful of desserts and an occasional glass of wine actually gave me the balance that I needed.**

What I found was that every individual must answer the question of "why would you" in a way that is personalized to him or her. Each of my teammates established her own parameters and limits for what was acceptable, and I had to do the same. The period of living The Mantra under The Rules with The Schedule allowed me to realize that I actually took my monk lifestyle to too much of an extreme. For me, a few extra pounds, a few swims and hikes, social time with family and friends, a handful of desserts and an occasional glass of wine actually gave me the balance that I needed.

From that point forward, I prided myself on being a cyclist with balance. My teammate Maura coined the term "Happiness Watts," which she described as the extra watts (i.e., power) that you get by doing activities that make you happy. Essentially, being happy makes one a better cyclist. She argues that "extremism has given way to the common misconception in racing that 'the more I suffer, the better I will perform.'

Amy Charity, El Salvador, 2014. "Race Weight!'"

In complete agreement with Maura's theory, I concluded that activities done in moderation will help you strike the necessary balance to optimize your potential. You have to be content to perform well. I encourage aspiring athletes to go ahead and eat that brownie, dance at your cousin's wedding, and spend time with your friends. Having mental balance and positive energy are a critical part of the success equation.

> **Having mental balance and positive energy are a critical part of the success equation.**

Everything in moderation, including moderation.
—Mark Twain

Understand the scale of discipline and balance.

Establish your own parameters.

If you're trying to reach your peak potential, trade-offs are inevitable. Now that you have made a concerted effort to live by a set of rules, and made it through your specified time frame, you may find that you have gone too far in some areas. Congratulations! This is a great lesson to learn—you have found your limits. It is critical to test your boundaries, and then ease off of the restrictions in the areas where you have gone too far. These boundaries are personal to every individual. For some, food restrictions, scheduling rules, lifestyle limitations are appropriate. For others, balance is the key to doing something well.

Suffering for the sake of suffering is a futile exercise. Find what works for you as an individual. Do not worry about the others that are training more, eating less, sleeping more, racing more, working longer hours, etc. It is easy to get caught up with competitors or other experts in your area. Have confidence that you are unique and that you have your own path to maximize your potential.

Maintaining perspective is not always easy when you are in the bubble of your dreams, and surrounded by people in the exact same echo chamber.

Find what works for you as an individual.

Complicating the matter is the question of why would you do anything that might hinder your ability to reach your potential? This line of thinking when taken to an extreme, can cause more harm than good.

PART IV

Step Away fromYour Comfort Zone

CHAPTER ELEVEN

You Could Be Happy Living in Jail

At War! (El Salvador)

We had strict instructions not to fall off the back of the pack during the bike race, because the country had one of the highest kidnapping rates in the world.

My lesson in adaptation arrived early in my pro cycling career, and became a theme. The pinnacle of adaptation was racing in El Salvador. In an ideal racing situation, I believe that preparation is everything. Adequate sleep, a balanced diet, rest, and mental focus are key ingredients to succeeding in a race. A common routine the day before a race would be the following: memorize the course; study the competitors; identify who I would mark; keep my legs up the entire day; drink beet juice; stay hydrated; and visualize a race win.

In the case of El Salvador, race preparation was categorically thrown out the window. Prior to this race, I operated under the assumption that there were a few basic human requirements that were essential and a given. Maslow defined these needs as physiological, i.e., food, water, warmth, and rest. The focus shifted to survival, and my teammates and I lived through two weeks of questionable standards related to accommodation, food, water, health, physical comfort and safety.

Due to the small budget of our cycling team, we were restricted on how much we could afford to bring to El Salvador. Upon arriving in this small Central American country, our race director informed us that the bike pump and race food did not make the cut. Although inconvenient, we could be resourceful and ask competing teams to help with any mechanical issues that we had with our bikes. Some of the larger budget teams arrived with mechanics, directors and soigneurs. This meant that those racers had a shot at rest and were able to focus more on racing and less on ensuring that they had the essentials to even show up to the race.

We knew that we would have to make friends and improvise. It was clear that the playing field would not be equal from a preparation standpoint. In the back of my head, I repeated what my dad used to tell me throughout my childhood: "Only worry about what you can control, the rest is out of your hands." Quite frankly, the lack of race and bike preparedness soon became the least of our concerns.

The pickup truck arrived at Monseñor Óscar Arnulfo Romero International Airport to take my teammates and I to our home for the upcoming two weeks of racing. My Spanish skills came in especially handy as I attempted to learn where we would stay. Our team had competed in the same race the previous year, and were fortunate to stay in a four-star hotel. We heard rumors of other teams staying in a substandard dorm that year, and we all crossed our fingers that we were back in the fancy hotel.

I quickly learned that our *Accommodation Fairy* was not looking over us in 2014. We arrived at the sports complex dorm building, which was wrapped in barbed wire and surrounded by security officers armed with machine guns patrolling the grounds 24/7. Essentially, we were on lockdown until we were released to ride.

We were provided with breakfast the first two mornings of the race, but woke up on the third morning to discover that breakfast would not be available. "*Lo siento, no hay comida,*" we were told. With ninety degree temperatures, my soggy PB and Js turned out to be less than ideal. We had to evaluate the lesser of two evils on a ninety-five degree day in a seventy-five mile race: taking water from neutral support and risk getting the stomach bug; wiping out the peloton; or go for dehydration.

Team Vanderkitten made every effort to avoid the illnesses that swept through the team the previous year that they competed in Vuelta Ciclista, El Salvador. We vowed to brush our teeth with filtered water, keep our mouths closed while showering, cook our own food, avoid vegetables at all costs, and resist taking water from anyone other than our team director. We understood the futility of our efforts when one of my teammates witnessed a staff member from the dorm fill the "filtered" water jug with a hose in the back of the building.

Remaining healthy, unfortunately, proved to be an unattainable challenge. Racing, especially for nine days, makes everyone susceptible to illness. The odds were against us from the start, as one of my teammates arrived in El Salvador ill. She did her best to avoid getting the rest of us sick, but the bug was inevitable.

My teammates, Kate and Miranda, and Director Jono weren't far behind in catching the El Salvadoran bug. One by one, each of my six teammates and I started to feel symptoms of different illnesses. The El Salvadoran race doctor visited each of us and took our pulses, felt our foreheads, and diagnosed us with various illnesses. "You have bronchitis, I am sure of it," he told my teammate/roommate in broken English, after listening to her cough. "You have pneumonia," he told another teammate after feeling her forehead. Despite the fact that we all had a mysterious El Salvadoran illness, we got up every morning like zombies to attempt to survive a seventy mile race.

We had strict instructions not to fall off the back of the pack during the bike race, because the country had one of the highest kidnapping rates in the world. Now that was a compelling reason to dig deep if I'd ever heard one (as you can see in my expression in this photo where I'm attempting to get back in the peloton after crashing in a tunnel)!

After El Salvador, I knew that I could survive any US racing scene and suboptimal environments prior to racing.

I ultimately concluded that racing for two weeks in El Salvador must be a small taste of what going to war feels like. In short, we all lived (except for the helicopter pilot, but that's a different story), we all came back sick, race-lean, and adequately prepared for anything that the US pro peloton could throw our way.

Amy chasing back onto the peloton, El Salvador

It was incredibly challenging to maintain perspective in those conditions. Prior to most bike races, I prided myself on meticulous preparation that included the hours of sleep I received the three nights leading up to a race, every calorie that I put into my body, my study of race bibles to understand exactly what I would encounter. All of that preparation

I was scared for my safety, my health, my well-being, and that of my teammates and friends.

went out the window in El Salvador, and my teammates and I had to rely on the minimal basics that we had. The positive memories from El Salvador were the support and kindness that we received from some of the local Salvadorans, the deep bonds of friendship that formed between a handful of the racers, and the knowledge that survival instincts come into play in trying times. After El Salvador, I knew that I could survive any US racing scene and suboptimal environments prior to racing.

I also began to understand the limits of one's Learning Zone. Clearly outside of my Comfort Zone, I pushed the boundaries of my Learning Zone in El Salvador and experienced moments and entire races in the Panic Zone. I had gone too far with discomfort, and no longer thrived in a new environment. I was scared for my safety, my health, my well-being, and that of my teammates and friends. Understand when you've gone too far, or when it is too much to even learn from the experience.

MENTAL STATE: *I crossed over the line of the Learning Zone and entered the Panic Zone.*

Vino for Lunch? (Tuscany)

Learning to roll with the punches continued to be a critical characteristic throughout my cycling career. Similar to El Salvador, the Tour of Tuscany proved to be an opportunity to test how adaptable my teammates and I could be.

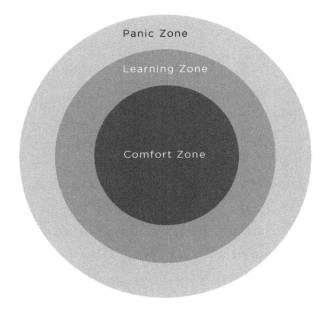

Cycling season was over. I had just wrapped up the Steamboat Springs Stage Race, the Labor Day weekend stage race that bookends the cycling season. My season kicked off in El Salvador seven months earlier, so I was ready for a break. That said, I then received an email from our team director:

Ladies, we've been invited to race the Tour of Tuscany. This would be an incredible opportunity to do a UCI race in Europe. No pressure, but it would be great if we could get a team to compete....

How could I resist! Not only was it an international race in one of the most famous cycling destinations in the world, but the quality of racers and racing would be incredibly high, representing Russia, Italy, Israel, Mexico, Colombia, Great Britain, and Belgium. Although at this point in my cycling career I was still paying to travel to races, I concluded that it was well worth the financial investment to race in Italy.

Before I knew it, I was heading back to Europe to compete with my trade team, Vanderkitten, a couple of guest riders, another US Domestic Elite team, and a strong racer from Switzerland. Doggedly pursuing any endeavor that supported my ultimate goal, I enthusiastically accepted an additional racing opportunity. Only eight days separated receiving the email from the team director to touching down in Florence.

Italians, and specifically the Fanini family that host the Tour of Tuscany race, have their special way of doing things. We did our best to embrace the culture, as appropriate, and roll with the punches. The stage race consisted of a short prolog and three additional stages. The two-kilometer prolog featured a pre-race celebratory lunch serving vats of pasta with marinara and Parmesan, white bread, and naturally, bottles of red and white wine. It wasn't exactly the pre-race meal of beet salad and Osmo Preload that American cyclists might have opted for. As much as I enjoy a glass of wine with pasta, I was well aware that the upcoming race agony would not improve with such a beverage choice.

Our team had mixed results and overcame challenges that are part of racing abroad and not having ideal resources or financial backing. Specifically, we arrived at the race without a time trial bike. The first stage, a prolog of three miles, made a time trial bike all but essential. We managed to borrow a bike from a bike shop in Lucca. The shortest girl on the team was 5'3" and the tallest, 5'9". By no stretch of the imagination is one TT bike ideal to accommodate our range of heights. However, that is exactly what this bike did.

I was the last of the six of us to race. My teammate finished eight minutes before my start time. She hopped off the bike and we pulled out the Allen key and quickly adjusted the saddle. I hopped on the bike and hustled to the starting line. In any other situation, I would have had every millimeter of the bike professionally fit. In this race, I was merely hoping that the saddle did not slip.

Throughout the Tour of Tuscany, there were endless factors that were out of our control from what we were fed, to how much time we had between arriving at the race and the race start. One of the days, we struggled to make our way through the one-way roads and tight alleys and did not have time to pump our tires before the race. On the start line, I felt mine and could tell by touch that it was much lower than optimal PSI.

> I can only control my personal preparation, my mindset, and my reaction.

My fears came true and within the first five miles of the race my tire deflated. I raised my hand, waved down neutral support and moved to the back of the peloton until I could get a wheel change. Making my way up through the caravan and back into the peloton, I realized immediately that my gears were not meshing correctly (I was riding a ten-speed bike and the cassette on the wheel was intended for an eleven-speed bike). As the gears jumped, I continued to ride on the heavy, misaligned wheel, knowing that I did not have another option.

With our mechanical issues and less-than-ideal preparation, my team-mates and I simply put our heads down, focused on doing the best we could, and just kept pedaling. My takeaway in Italy, similar to El Salvador, revealed that I will not always have control over circumstances. I can only control my personal preparation, my mindset, and my reaction. Remaining calm, calling on strength of character not to make a scene, not to panic, but to do the best I could under the circumstances proved to be a powerful lesson applicable in many aspects of life outside of bike racing.

Sleeping at the Airport to Becoming National Champions

At the age of thirty-eight, spending >100 nights away from home was challenging. The accommodation ranged from comfortable, to borderline seedy and undoubtedly cramped. Women's cycling is not a high-budget sport. Typically, we reached out to families in the towns where we would race, and requested host (aka free) housing. Essentially, two to eight female racers would take over the home of some generous and willing individual or family.

Host houses ranged from absolutely perfect, such as White Rock, British Columbia, where

Prepare to the best of your ability, and adapt to what you cannot control.

I had my own room, bathroom and a view of the ocean, to where I had an aero mattress, lined up next to my teammates' aero mattresses. Under no circumstance is a deflating AeroBed, with a cat snuggled on your legs, and a snoring teammate within an arm's length an ideal environment for the night before the race.

Regardless, these host housing experiences became one of my favorite aspects of bike racing. Not only did they teach us about adapting, but some of the enduring relationships stemmed from these stays. Every May I looked forward to my trip to Chattanooga, where Ali and Spencer took me and my teammates into their home with open arms. They stocked up on every imaginable food that cyclists could ever desire, borrowed mattresses from their parents and neighbors and would go completely out of their way to make our stay comfortable and enjoyable.

Lauren Roos, in Redlands, demonstrated the same level of hospitality cooking meals for my teammate Kate and I, and creating private, comfortable spaces in her home for us to relax between stages.

Host housing varied dramatically and we all learned to show up prepared for anything. I traveled to every race with an eye mask and headphones as race essentials, and made the most of noise, temperature, mattress, lighting, that I encountered. The race essentials came in especially handy the night that my teammate, Jasmine, and I slept on the floor of George Bush Intercontinental Airport. In case you have not had this pleasure, it turns out that the night staff blares music in the wee hours of the night. You guessed it—country music and it was loud. They do not distribute blankets, although that would have been nice given the temperature fluctuated between 55-60 degrees Fahrenheit. Not typically one to spoon, I found myself cuddled up to Jasmine for warmth, counting down the minutes until the Starbucks would open at five a.m. so I could get a hot drink.

Twenty-four hours later, my teammates and I became the 2015 National Champions.

The entire flight debacle was completely out of our control. Somehow, we managed to keep it together and not let the setbacks affect us mentally. I knew that I had the most important race of my life twenty-four hours after leaving the Houston airport. I could control my nutrition, my rest, my thoughts, and therefore my mental state. I kept my legs up in the airport and dreamt about winning the National Championship.

USA Team Time Trial 2015 Champions. Left to Right Leah Kirchmann, Jasmine Glaesser, Alison Tetrick, Amy Charity, Brianna Walle, Annie Ewart

Twenty-four hours later, my teammates and I became the 2015 National Champions. I relay the story with a fondness of the bonding that might have just helped our team achieve victory. With these genuinely positive thoughts, my best friend Jenny often remarks, "Amy, I'm fairly certain you would be happy living in jail!"

MENTAL STATE: *The time I spent outside of my comfort zone led to one of the most fulfilling moments that I have ever experienced.*

> **Character cannot be developed in ease and quiet. Only through experience of trial and suffering can the soul be strengthened, ambition inspired, and success achieved.**
> —Helen Keller

Prepare for the worst.

Be resilient. Adapt and learn.

In striving to accomplish your goals, know that everything will not go as planned. Regardless of how prepared you are, some decisions or outcomes will fall out of your control. The key is to prepare for what you can and adapt to the changes.

You cannot control many of the events that happen to you, and you may not be in control of the final outcome. That said, you are in control of your calmness, maturity, and reaction to unexpected situations.

Understand what you are willing to put up with; understand what you may need to put up with. Try to embrace the situation, knowing that it won't last forever.

Prepare to the best of your ability, and adapt to what you cannot control. Try to enjoy the ride!

> **When, not if, things are not going to plan, it is your reaction and how you handle the situation that matters.**

CHAPTER TWELVE

The Art of Perseverance

The Answer Is No (x 1,000)

To my sheer surprise and disappointment,
my name did not appear on the list.

I've always wondered who holds the world record on being told no. I think I may be up for contention for the award. At the very least, I must be a member of the long list. Professional cycling, similar to anything where you are competing with the best, can be a humbling endeavor. I have been told "no" more times that I can count. In addition to building character, the process eventually allowed me to accomplish my goals.

The first year that I rose through the ranks in the Colorado cycling scene, winning the Colorado Road and Criterium State Championships in the Category 1 & 2 field, I thought I might have a shot at making it on a national level. I sent my resume to the directors of every domestic elite team in the US. I heard back from one.

"Impressive resume. How old are you?" the director asked.

> **I was told no again and again and again, and yet managed to accomplish more than I ever thought possible.**

"Thirty-four," I answered.

"My apologies, but your age will skew our team average too much. Best of luck to you," she kindly replied.

Essentially, I was told that I was too old from the one person who took the time to acknowledge my request. I didn't even hear back from any of the others!

The "no's" that I received continued throughout my cycling career. Below are some of my favorites:

MINIMAL RACING: In my first-year racing for Vanderkitten, I was told that I wouldn't be able to do many races with the team and would be an alternate.

- *Action:* I worked my tail off throughout the season. I calmly and rationally spoke to the director about how I could contribute to the team and how each particular race suited my strengths. I remained a good teammate to the other women on the team. I offered to pay my own way to travel to the races.

- *Outcome:* I raced 70 days my first year on Vanderkitten.

ROSTER IS ALREADY FILLED. I was given a definitive no from the Director of Optum, informing me that they had filled all of their spots for the 2015 racing year.

- *Action*: I worked my tail off throughout the offseason ensuring that I would be fit. I made alternate plans for another team, yet stayed in contact with the team director as well as the team members.

- *Outcome*: I was a proud team member of Optum Professional Women's Racing Team for the 2015 racing year.

NOT SUITED FOR TEAM USA. I was told: "You are more of a hill climber; the USA National team takes women who *race* their bikes!"

- *Action*: I worked my tail off. I remained in contact with the Director of the USA National Team. I listened to exactly what it takes to be successful racing in Europe (extermely hard, three-hour, 2,400 kilojoule rides) and my coach and I developed a plan to ensure I could handle European racing.

- *Outcome*: I raced in Europe for the USA National Team in 2014 and 2015 (and was on the podium in a UCI race).

NOT RACING TTT. I was told that I would not be on Optum's Time Trial Team, as they had recruited racers specifically for that race and I was not one of them.

- *Action*: I worked my tail off. I attended the TTT camps. I built time into training on my time trial bike two days per week to ensure that I could maximize output in a tight aero position.

- *Outcome*: My teammates and I won the National Championship in the Team Time Trial.

NOT RACING WORLDS TTT. I was told that although I had raced on the Team Time Trial team for Nationals, I would not be on the Worlds team.

- *Action*: I worked my tail off. I continued to work almost exclusively on improving my power on the time trial bike. I practiced team time trials with my coach and my husband and other strong riders who challenged me. I motor paced on a regular basis to get comfortable staying millimeters from a wheel (bumper) at high speeds (30-plus mph).

- *Outcome*: I raced the World Championships in Richmond in 2015.

I was told no again and again and again, and yet managed to accomplish more than I ever thought possible. It turns out that I was not too old, too meek, or too inexperienced to race at the top level of women's cycling. I had the confidence and the belief that I was good enough, so I put my head down and just kept riding. Despite my age and lack of experience, I managed to go further than I ever thought possible in bike racing.

The common denominator in the five scenarios I've shared is that of continuously working hard. I never quit; I never accepted a "no" at face value. I found ways to push through the discouragement and remain hopeful that I still had a shot.

Alternative Options

Pacing my house, I waited anxiously for the email to arrive from our team director informing us of the roster for the upcoming European races. Coming off of a high from our team's success at the Tour of California the previous week, I felt strong, fit, and confident. I finished the race 11th in GC and had a couple of top ten finishes in the stages. I was in good form and knew that I had contributed to our team leader's success.

Finally, the email appeared in my inbox. I quickly scrolled through the names for the Tour of Britain. Chest tightening, I re-read the email a few times to ensure that I hadn't missed anything. To my sheer surprise and disappointment, my name did not appear on the list. My mind raced with all of the potential reasons why I had not been selected. Understanding the team director's personality, I realized that calling and begging was not an option. In my next conversation with him, I could simply ask why; however, at that point, the decision had been made.

> I had the confidence and the belief that I was good enough, so I put my head down and just kept riding.

The source of my disappointment stemmed from my close connection to England, and the fact that I felt that I had been one of the strongest on the team in the first half of the racing season. I had already anticipated flying to my husband's home country, seeing my in-laws and my English friends, treating myself to some treacle sponge pudding (after a race win). I hadn't even considered that I wouldn't be part of the Tour of Britain squad. I felt like I had been punched in the gut as I read the email. Although there are never guarantees in which races one will participate, I had completely planned on heading to Europe for several weeks in July. Unfortunately, that is not what the director had in mind for me. He could only take six racers out of a team of eleven, and I was not one of them.

Crushed, I knew I had to make the best of the situation. I required a long ride to relieve stress, clear my mind, and reset my thinking. Pedaling through the rolling hills, my thoughts transitioned through all of the emotional stages of disappointment—sadness, disbelief, and eventually to acceptance. By the end of the ride, I felt okay, and ready to take on an alternate plan. I reminded myself of the races I had already done and took the time to really feel good about how far I had come in my cycling career. From there, I mapped out a training plan with my coach to ensure that I would be adequately prepared for the next races.

Finally, I talked to the director to discuss an alternative racing plan for that period of time. My coach, director and I eventually landed on BC Superweek in Canada as my next race. While the short duration, technical, fast-pace criteriums did not exactly suit my racing strengths, it would be a great opportunity for building skills with a solid week of racing criteriums.

It's not always feasible to simply keep asking, or to ask the question in a different way. On many occasions, I was told no and had to make the best of alternative options. These small setbacks allowed me to reconnect with my original goals and the big picture.

Fall down seven times, get up eight.
—Japanese Proverb

MENTAL STATE: *I have moved outside of my Comfort Zone and am in the Learning Zone.*

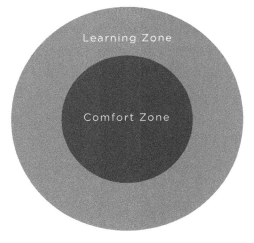

Rejection becomes motivation.

The art of perseverance is understanding what your options are, and to continue moving toward your goals. You always need to be strategically thinking through options, while keeping the big picture in the back of your head.

Persevere when you are told no.

If you are told no, think through an alternate method of asking that may change the outcome. Reach out to the person, understanding where he or she is coming from, and letting him or her know why you think you are the most qualified. Suggest a compromise that might still allow you to move in the direction that you need to, and will also work for the person you're asking. Perhaps it's appropriate to ask someone else. I'm not suggesting playing the old "Mom said no, ask Dad" trick that many of us mastered as kids, but the idea of speaking to a different person with a similar request could be advantageous.

Finally, you may ask again after you improve your value proposition. Perhaps you take time to become more qualified. Perhaps you offer something in exchange for what person is giving you. Be creative and you just might find a solution that meets everyone's needs.

The beauty of having a strong passion is that the rejection you encounter isn't necessarily a blow to the gut. If you are passionate about your endeavor and believe in your abilities, then setbacks can actually fuel the fire and increase your motivation for success.

CHAPTER THIRTEEN

The Unknowns

*One of the most challenging
aspects of the sport for me was
the lack of certainty.*

There are endless examples of women in the pro field who have made it to the top teams because of their willingness to persevere and continue when things aren't necessarily going as they planned. There were certainly times, especially in my first two years of racing for Vanderkitten, that I considered leaving the sport. What some imagine might be the hardest parts of the professional racing lifestyle, such as the endless training hours, the time away from home, the insufficient (or nonexistent) salary, etc., were not what I considered to be the hardest parts of professional bike racing.

One of the most challenging aspects of the sport for me was the lack of certainty. In the corporate world, I always had a fairly good idea of where I stood and what I could expect in the upcoming weeks, months, or even years. I had semi-annual reviews, with a clearly documented pay scale based on performance metrics and job responsibilities. However, women's professional cycling is essentially the antithesis of organized and predictable corporate culture.

In women's professional racing, ninety percent of the women sign one-year contracts. The result is that if you win a stage in a competitive international racing field, you might be recruited to a different (higher ranking) team for the following race season. For example, in 2015 one of my teammates won two stages and finished second overall at an early season prestigious UCI race. Impressed with her strong result, a director from a competing team began negotiating a contract with this teammate for the following year. From my perspective, we were just starting to work well together as a team. Meanwhile, a seed had been planted in her mind about the following year, and who her teammates might be at that point. The uncertainty around contracts and racing teams is exacerbated for domestiques who serve as the support crew for their team leader. At the end of a race, the domestique's contribution isn't always clear.

I certainly didn't know how the following year would unfold regarding a contract and a team, nor did I have certainty around which races I would even participate in the upcoming weeks or months. Most races allowed six riders per team to participate, thus leaving half of the team out of the race. The guidance I followed was to remain fit and ready. At any point, I would receive a call from the team director informing me that I would be flying out of DIA in a few days to participate in the upcoming race, which could be anywhere in the US or Europe.

As someone who emerged from corporate culture, naturally planned ahead and appreciated some control over her whereabouts, I found the uncertainty challenging. A few suboptimal results, health issues, or an injury had a dramatic effect on a cyclist's fate for upcoming races and for the following year. Given all of the unknowns in the sport, I had to continuously remind myself of the end goal of racing in the top level of my sport, and how fortunate I was to be in a position to pursue my passion. Most importantly, I had to let go of all of the decisions that were not in my control. I could control my attitude, my demeanor, my preparation and my training.

MENTAL STATE:

I have moved outside of my Comfort Zone and am in the Learning Zone.

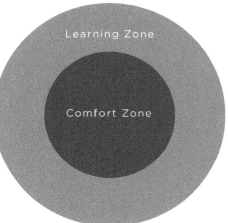

Let go of what you can't control.

ACCEPT THE UNKNOWNS. There are many situations that will be out of your control, and this can be challenging. Most of us are accustomed to having the authority to make decisions that determine our next course of action. Identify all of the actions and outcomes that you can control and ensure that you are doing everything within your power to move toward your goals.

- *You determine how you react when something happens to you.*
- *You decide if you want to evaluate a situation with optimism or pessimism. You manage your thought process.*
- *You make the decision to stay the course when something is not going how you planned.*

Courage is the power to let go of the familiar.
—Raymond Lindquist

Although there may be decisions that you are not directly administering, ensure that you respond in a way that you are comfortable for those decisions that you can control. Bring yourself back to your original goal and recognize that it is going to require more perseverance than you may have originally thought.

CHAPTER FOURTEEN

Bordering the Learning and Panic Zones

The Beastly Dutchies

When you are nervous and have the jitters, and aren't sure if you can complete the task ahead of you, recognize that everything that you have done in your life has prepared you for this moment.

In January 2015, I received an email from Jack Seehafer, USA National Team Women's Director, asking me to race the Spring Classics in Europe with the US National Team. In summary, it is a once-in-a-lifetime opportunity to race some of the most prestigious races in the world, where only the top teams in the world are invited, and they race against the strongest cyclists in the female peloton. Even more meaningful is the chance to race for the National Team. There is nothing more motivating than putting on a stars and stripes jersey, and teaming up with a few of the most talented racers in the US.

Additionally, we had the opportunity to race under the guidance of legendary Ina Yoko Teutenberg, which is nothing short of an honor.

With her extensive and successful cycling history, Ina's Palmarès proved that she was one of the most talented and successful female cyclists over the past two decades. An Olympian and the champion of some of the most prestigious races in the world, Ina knows just about everything there is to know about races, racers, tactics, suffering, etc. I knew that she would have a great deal to offer, and I suspected that she would be tough.

> **The skills of these Europeans were something for which I aspired, and at the time, settled on admiration and awe.**

Racing in Europe would represent new and unknown challenges in bike racing that I could not even begin to imagine without being there to experience it. The infamous Block One with USA cycling might be considered the most challenging trip that the National Team takes to Europe, notorious for cobbles, high winds, enormous field sizes, narrow roads, heavy rain, crashes, road furniture, and feisty Euros, especially the Beastly Dutchies who are ready to display their early season fitness and aggression. American women are not known for being small, but when placed in the middle of a European group of female cyclists, it is difficult to see above or even around the Dutch women. Their skills are jaw-dropping, and their size is intimidating, to say the least.

> **I knew I had to dig deep into my mental toughness and keep myself together prior to the start of the race.**

The scene forever ingrained in my mind is riding at twenty-five mph, shoulder to shoulder with women on both sides, in a pack of 180 racers. Millimeters in front of me, the next wheel. I could barely grab a drink from my water bottle without touching someone. Did I mention that the group moved at a pace of twenty-five mph or faster? The unbelievable part was that some of these beastly giants actually made their way up to the front of the group by riding through the middle of the pack. To be clear, there was not room. By extending my arm, I could have easily made contact with about nine women. That is how close we raced. The skills of these Europeans were something for which I aspired, and at the time, settled on admiration and awe.

All of the challenges aside, racing in Europe is a cyclist's dream. Racing with large crowds of spectators filling the towns to cheer on their cycling heroes is a cyclist's version of playing in the Super Bowl. Helicopters fly above to capture television footage of the racing, and fans swarm the cyclists before and after the races, hoping to capture a picture, an autograph, or an esteemed used water bottle.

The Belgians bring photo albums that contain every UCI racing roster, which includes every professional women's racing team in the world. They collect and carry Pro Cards (similar to baseball cards) with the racer's picture, weight, height, hometown, date of birth, nationality, sponsors, etc. In the US, my mom and a few members of my close inner circle had

a copy of my Pro Card. In Belgium, I had several strangers walk up to me and ask for my autograph on a copy of my picture printed from our team's website. I was in utter disbelief. Obviously flattered, but more importantly, I was completely blown away by the level of interest in women's racing in Europe.

To my surprise, I was asked to sign my Pro Card in Belgium by collectors.

Needless to say, European bike racing culture is dramatically different than US bike racing. The energy is electric and the races are intense. This new racing environment is almost enough to make one have a mental breakdown on the start line. Knees shaking, mouth quivering, stomach churning, I could barely function or answer basic questions my teammates asked. Clearly a long way from being comfortable, I knew I had to dig deep into my mental toughness and keep myself together prior to the start of the race. I will always remember Heather Fischer calming my fears on the start line when I would tell her, "I want to do well. This is a UCI race and it is being televised!"

"Yes, and you have raced before and you have raced in big groups before," she responded. "You know exactly what to do. We discussed the team tactics in our meeting last night. You have a specific role. You have ridden in hundreds of races and tens of thousands of miles. You are ready. All of your preparation has led you to this moment. Enjoy the ride. You'll do great and all of your teammates are here with you."

I loved her optimism, her logic, and her support. I try to cast my mind back to her message anytime I am nervous about what I am about to do.

All progress takes place outside the comfort zone.
—Michael John Bobak

Team USA in Czech Republic. Front row: Brianna Walle, Kendall Ryan, Heather Fischer, Amy Charity, Abby Mickey, Lauren Decrescenzo, Back row: lodging host (left), Jack Seehafer (middle)

You are ready for this moment!

Persevere when you are completely terrified.

When you are nervous and have the jitters, and aren't sure if you can complete the task ahead of you, recognize that everything that you have done in your life has prepared you for this moment. You are ready—whether it is giving a presentation, walking into a job interview, or competing in a race. Apply logical reasoning and don't let your mind wander off to the possibilities of what might not go well. You know what to do. Let the nerves that you have fuel you to do well. Leverage the energy circulating through your body. Direct your thoughts to the positives: You have prepared; you are competent; you are capable; and you will do well.

CHAPTER FIFTEEN

Grinta
(= Grit in Italian)

Get Back on Your Bike

*To my dismay, most crashes left me
in the bone-breaking camp,
rather than the road rash camp.*

One valuable lesson I learned racing in Europe, revealing a new aspect of grit that I hadn't previously embraced was post-crash protocol. The risk of crashing is inevitable and a very real part of bike racing. In my three years of professional racing I separated a shoulder, had two concussions, broke my elbow, and hit the pavement for road rash and bone bruises more times than I can count. I was actually one of the racers who had fewer crashes than most!

Crashes are often unavoidable when there are 100-200 women trying to get to the same position in the pack with high winds, roads with potholes and/or lawn furniture, all traveling more than twenty-five mph, and touching elbows.

Crashes can be nasty enough to leave one with a Traumatic Brain Injury (TBI), or broken bones.

Regardless, they are a very realistic risk every time a racer rolls up to the start line.

The unbelievable part of bike racing is how many cyclists pick themselves up off of the pavement and continue the race. I learned this basic lesson to "brush it off" and get back on the bike while racing some of the most mentally and physically challenging races that I had ever experienced.

Historically, my crashes have resulted in up to six weeks off the bike, broken bones, torn ligaments, and cracked helmets. A high-speed crash with no real injury was a whole new world to me. Although I had been warned about the "death cracks" in the Omloop Het Hageland course, I managed to dive my wheel straight into a crack that was parallel to the road, i.e., a 25mm bike tire fits perfectly into the crack that is running the same direction that we are riding. From head down in agony, trying to close the gap on the wheel that was a few yards in front of me to laying on the pavement was a matter of indiscernible seconds.

My series of events went something along the lines of:

1 Lay in the road and think. I'm on the ground, but I'm not dead. Phew!

2 Get up.

3 Note that chain is off and slowly put it back on.

4 Note that jersey is torn and my bum is hanging out of torn shorts.

5 Get back on bike and see that most of the caravan has passed.

6 Start chasing after caravan in vain.

My race, Omloop Het Hageland Tielt-Winge, was over. Ina, the race director for this particular race, advised me of the proper protocol, which consisted not of six steps, but rather two.

1 Check your body, head and bike (in one simultaneous and quick motion)!

2 Get back on your bike, ride like hell, get back in the group (in a second fast and simultaneous motion)

Unfortunately, that wasn't exactly my reaction.

I cannot count the number of times that one who hit the pavement at high speeds actually becomes the race winner in the same race. My teammate, Annie Ewart, managed this famous move in Stage Two of the Tour of the Gila in 2015. It shows a level of grit and perseverance in its purest form. The physical demands of a bike race are already immeasurable. Combine that with a sore knee or shoulder and blood trickling down your arm and there is the clearest example of grit that I have ever known. It's even discussed regularly among cyclists. "When you know you're about to crash, you have to just go floppy," my Australian teammate, Miranda, would tell me. "If you don't go floppy, you'll break a bone." "Land on the big soft spots," fellow racers advised. "You're less likely to break a wrist, hand, or collarbone if you land on your bum." To my dismay, most crashes left me in the bone-breaking camp, rather than the road rash camp.

After crashing at Omloop Het Hageland, luckily with no broken bones, I was left

You need to get back on your bike and win the race.

with road rash on my left shoulder that was moderately painful. After each conversation that I had with Ina, she would pat me on my left shoulder.

"Owww!" I'd gasp, feeling the sharp pain of the road rash.

"Oops," she would reply, impishly.

Later I asked the mechanic, Mirik: "Why do you think Ina keeps smacking my left arm? Has she forgotten that I have road rash? Could she not hit my right arm instead?"

Belgium Race: Omloop Het Hageland. Amy Charity post crash.

"Amy," Mirik replied in his serious and stoic tone, "you need to get back on your bike and win the race. Then, Ina will hit your right arm—the one without road rash."

> **The world breaks everyone,
> and afterward, some are strong
> at the broken places.**
> —Ernest Hemingway

That Little Bit Extra

One must have a certain level of talent, but the hard worker is the one to watch out for. The Italians brilliantly use the word "grinta" to describe grit and drive. Racing the Tour of Tuscany in Italy, the cheer that I heard repeatedly was "grinta, grinta" as I made my way up the long climbs.

In addition to hard work and drive, the other dimension of the "grit" equation, that my fellow bike racers and I discuss at length, is the ability to suffer. Bike racing is always hard. However, there is a point when it goes beyond hard to borderline intolerable. It is when every muscle fiber is screaming, your lungs are burning, your vision is blurry, and you know that all of the pain will disappear instantly if you just lessen the pressure on the pedals.

> **One must have a certain level of talent, but the hard worker is the one to watch out for.**

A select few cyclists emerge and the real race begins at that point. A handful of cyclists, demonstrating such a high level of grit, will push through the agony and find strength in their depleted bodies to fight for a few more seconds on the wheel in front of them.

Is it pushing through to a level that you never dreamed possible?

What is it that enables one to push beyond any reasonable limit of what a human can do?

Does she have the highest pain tolerance in the group?

Does she want the end result more than anyone else?

Is she the strongest mentally?

I believe that it is a combination of all of the above.

Stillwater, MN, Race: North Star Gran Prix. Amy Charity suffering.

If you are going through hell, keep going.
—Winston Churchill

Just Hang On!

Undoubtedly, bike racing will bring out grit and courage that one may not know that she even has. In one of my last races as a Professional, the Pro Cycling Challenge in Colorado, my limits of courage were put to the test.

Within the first ten miles of the road race, I could feel my handlebars slipping down. I looked down again to see that my Garmin was literally pointing toward the ground. I knew I had to resolve this mechanical quickly as the attacks were just beginning. I put my hand up and the race commissure called the team car up to me. I explained to our director and mechanic what was happening. While hanging onto the car window, the mechanic attempted to fix my handlebars.

Eventually they decided that I would need to use my spare bike (which are all carried on the roof of the team car) while they fixed my race bike. They pulled over, we swapped bikes, and I made my way through the caravan back into the peloton. This effort can be exhausting. Some cyclists have mastered this skill and efficiently roll from bumper to bumper to get back into the race.

In one of my last races as a Professional, the Pro Cycling Challenge in Colorado, my limits of courage were put to the test.

Even in my last race, I was not completely comfortable with being in the caravan. I rode on my spare bike for approximately five miles and realized that the wheels were heavy and it wasn't as comfortable as my race bike. I knew with the upcoming climbs that I would only have a shot if I were on the right bike. I put my hand in the air and eventually made my way back to the caravan to get back on my race bike. The director pulled over to the side of the road and we quickly did the second bike swap. Attacks must have happened in the peloton because the caravan and peloton were gone.

Side Note: A practice that is considered acceptable in almost all professional racing circles, is for team cars to bring cyclists back into the race if they are out resulting from no fault of their own, such as a mechanical. If, on the other hand, I were off the back of the peloton because I couldn't keep up with the group, then getting assistance from the team car is absolutely cheating. I feel comfortable in my decision to get back to the group after having an issue with my bike.

I was doing everything I could not to panic.

Getting back to the group, even with assistance, is easier said than done. As I hung onto the passenger side window frame with my left hand, I hung onto my handlebars with my right hand. I kept my legs still and my knees fairly close together. Every feature on the road was flying by at speeds that I had never experienced on my bike. I was doing everything I could not to panic. I knew that anything—literally anything—in the road in front of my bike would end my life at the speed I was travelling. I started to shout to my director that I was okay, we were almost there, I could catch the group. I eventually let go of the window, fought my way to the front of the cars and eventually back into the group. The effort just to get back to where I had left the peloton burned too many matches for me to finish the race with a top result.

It wouldn't be until uploading my file later that night that I realized I had hit sixty-two mph hanging onto a car window.

Fight for it.

Ensure you care about what you're fighting for.

Successful people all have grit—something extra. There are many theories and studies on what makes one "gritty" and it has become a buzzword recently in defining success potential.

In her intriguing book, *Grit: The Power of Passion and Perseverance,* Angela Duckworth (Peguin, 2015) defines grit as an equation that "counts effort twice," i.e., "Talent x effort = skill. Skill x effort = achievement." After years of research on a range of people from cadets to children to musicians, she concludes that putting in the effort is more important than skill or talent alone. Passion and persistence are the keys to achievement.

The equation, broken down, suggests that passion—the desire, the belief, the pure enjoyment—is an essential part of the success potential. At the crux, you really have to want it. Although this may seem obvious, really think through what you want so badly that you are willing to suffer, to degrees that you never imagined possible, to reach what you are striving for. Think through examples of people who you have observed, who have wanted something so badly that they were able to take the win, get the promotion, or pass the exam, even if they were not as talented as their competitors.

The second part of the equation is persistence, which entails the mindset of never giving up. Demonstrating an unwavering level of commitment, the one who continues to chip away at her weaknesses and improve her strengths over weeks, months, or years is the one who prevails.

Passion and persistence are the keys to achievement.

To achieve anything, you have to fight for it. This fight is both physical and mental. Typically, the mental side is the greater challenge than the physical, even in a sport as physically demanding as bike racing. What you learn throughout the process is just how good it feels when you find success after the hard fight.

Courage is being scared to death, but saddling up anyway.
—John Wayne

PART V

Relationships

CHAPTER SIXTEEN

A Few Good Women

In addition to perseverance,
the essential characteristic that the
standout women in professional
racing share is integrity.

I f I had to boil down the hundreds of races in which I
competed, and the thousands of miles I pedaled through
various states and countries, and choose one word that defined
the experience and made it worthwhile, it would be relationships.
Now that some time has passed since my last race, I realize
even more how crucial and meaningful the friendships and
relationships were that I developed. Bike racing ultimately came
down to the characters in the sport and my interactions with them.
My details of race outcomes and feelings of agony are beginning to blur
together, but the strong bonds of friendship remain vivid.

In addition to perseverance, the essential characteristic that the standout
women in professional racing share is integrity. Similar to most sports,
truth of character is inevitably revealed at some point in bike racing.

Just the fact that they are in the sport, cyclists must be competitive. However, there are a few standouts who, based on their inherent characteristic of integrity, have proven to be successful as cyclists and will likely continue to find success throughout their lives. I learned to value the leaders, comics, caregivers and balance seekers. I tried to surround myself by the teammates and friends who possessed these character traits.

Leaders such as Leah Kirchmann, Alexis Ryan, and Heather Fisher, for example, always seemed to find a way to convey a message or a race tactic in a non-condescending and knowledgeable manner. These were teammates for whom you would slay yourself because you knew that they would do the same to get a win for the team. Even after horribly disappointing results, they would maintain composure and have a reassuring presence on the team.

> Another critical characteristic in the mix are the comics who keep the mood of the team elevated.

Leah, for example, encapsulated characteristics of a leader well beyond her twenty-five years. Poised, confident, humble yet self-assured, and grateful are a few of the many positive traits that Leah possessed. She treated teammates equally and with respect. Although this may seem fundamental, this trait certainly was not the norm among race leaders. Leah did not place blame when the leadout did not go as planned. She asked questions, understood how we could improve, and developed solutions. I admired her composure in high stress situations and she consistently shared success with the team, acknowledging the efforts of the team in any race.

Another critical characteristic in the mix are the comics who keep the mood of the team elevated. Brie Walle and Lauren Decrescendo will always stand out in my mind as ones who could lighten a mood, and get everyone in the room to laugh, regardless of how low we all felt.

Lauren was the girl who would blare rap or hip hop music an hour before a race and get everyone around her to start an impromptu dance party. Not only did we loosen up, relieve stress and tension, but she would have us in uncontrollable fits of laughter with her enthusiastic dance moves, her unmistakable memory of the lyrics, and her genuine encouragement to get everyone to join her.

Brie's contagious laugh, universal acceptance of every person, and unfaltering ability to see positive in every situation, kept the mood of the team uplifted regardless of race outcomes. Brie loved to talk, and had interesting stories about her stint in Germany and ski racing past. But as much as she loved to talk, her real talent was listening. She asked probing questions of teammates, friends and strangers alike.

One of my favorite memories in all of my racing years is the transfer (i.e., drive) from the Czech Republic to Belgium. Team USA had just won the stage race, Tour de Feminin, and my teammates and I felt that indistinguishable high of winning a bike race. The prospect of our upcoming five-hour journey did not quell our enthusiasm. Our next destination, the USA Cycling House located in the Netherlands, extended this European racing adventure.

Jack, tapping into his internal need for speed, embraced the Autobahn's unrestricted speed allowances with pure joy. In the back seat, Brie and I laughed uncontrollably the first time we saw the sign "Ausfahrt." After seeing it more than fifty times, and realizing that it meant "exit" in German, we continued to chuckle, or at least crack a smile every-single-time we passed the sign. I've come to learn that these memories are priceless, and some of the best of the entire racing experience.

The caregivers—Tiffany Pezzulo, Miranda Griffiths, Jennifer Reither, and Annie Ewart—were the women who looked after all of us, taking genuine interest in how their teammates were feeling, at a core level.

Their natural tendencies to be nurturing was not necessarily a result of age. Annie, for example, was the youngest on our team. I was always shocked at the reminder that she was in her early twenties. To put that in perspective, without too much of a stretch, I could have easily been her mother! That said, I completely relied on her extensive race experience and her general wisdom to guide me through tough situations in races and with the team dynamics.

Similar to Annie, Tiff had that nurturing instinct to take care of her teammates. She did this in a manner that portrayed ease, comfort and intuition. Sometime in the midst of racing disappointments, team confusion, financial frustration, and life questioning, I fortuitously spent two nights at Tiffany's home in Salt Lake City, Utah.

We sat at her kitchen counter, enjoying a few glasses of wine, cheese and crackers, authentic pasta, salad, and dessert. It was almost as if we were normal women in our thirties on a Friday night! Tiff's toddler ran around the house like any other two year old banging pots, making noise and giggling (incidentally, she is one of three women in the entire female professional peloton with a child), while Tiff casually cooked dinner. Seamlessly attending to her child's needs, clipping greens out of her garden for the salad, snacking on appetizers, Tiff managed to walk me off the proverbial cliff! In a time that I had just started to question what I had been thinking to leave my professional career, Tiff reminded me why this bike racing journey was worth it.

Although Tiff and I are similar ages, she is wise beyond her years and offered a humorous and thought-provoking perspective on how to make it work as a racing cyclist. Tiffany left a successful career as a lawyer in her late thirties to have better balance with her family and bike racing. Not only an icon for her criterium racing success, she found a way to juggle a complicated adult life with professional racing. She encouraged me to buy Phil Gaimon's book *Pro Cycling on $10 a Day,* to let go of what I could not control, and to occasionally enjoy some of the known "vices"— such as wine, gluten indulgences and dessert. Her positive encouragement and clear logical advice were instrumental in getting me back on track with my ultimate cycling goals.

Finally, there were those that helped keep us all in balance, ensuring that although we were professional athletes, we were allowed to have a bit of fun every now and then. Alison Tetrick and Maura Kinsella hold the candle for these traits. I recall that Alison brought Maura and me a glass of wine the night before the Tour of California to calm our nerves and celebrate our accomplishments of simply racing the Tour of California. As Alison handed me a glass of wine, I remember thinking, "Is this allowed? Is this a good idea? Will this prevent any of us from doing our jobs the next day?" I then let go of my inner monk, and reminded myself that "happiness watts" would play a role in this situation.

> Simply relaxing and bonding with teammates, and even celebrating being at the Tour of California, were the most important actions at that moment.

Simply relaxing and bonding with teammates, and even celebrating being at the Tour of California, were the most important actions at that moment. It turns out that our team had a phenomenal race, with Leah finishing seconds off of the overall winner. The rest of the team executed as planned setting her up for success throughout the race. Alison's gesture is one that I will never forget, and is a great reminder of the importance of simple acts of friendship.

Alison had many more racing years in her legs than I did, and I learned the importance of celebrating success and enjoying the moment with friends and teammates. Even in Fayetteville, Arkansas, after modest race success at the Joe Martin Stage Race, Alison encouraged us to honor the professional cyclist tradition of "Burger Sunday" (started by teammate Maura, and successfully embraced and celebrated by most of the women's racing teams!).

We asked our host mom for the best place to get a burger in Fayetteville and we found ourselves at the local Red Robin. Amused by the situation, the Optum ladies made the best of it and had one of those nights that reminded me why I loved the racing lifestyle. My teammates and I indulged in the burgers, a couple of beers, and sheer laughter driven by host housing oddities, stage race exhaustion, and racing memories.

Alison taught all of us the art of working hard and playing hard. Bike racing, although the center of our world, did not cure cancer or save lives. Ali mastered the switch from intense focus, game-on, shredding legs (as they say), to pure relaxation, laughter, and celebration. I will forever be grateful for her lessons on balance and living in the moment.

Observe characteristics that you admire. Emulate.

Observe behaviors of those around you. Seek those that are successful in your area of interest.

> *How do they behave?*
>
> *What do they do when thrown a curveball?*
>
> *How do they react? How do they treat people?*
>
> *How do they make others feel?*
>
> *How do you feel when you are around them?*

Take note of their behaviors and learn from them.

> **Don't walk through life just being an athlete.**
> **Athletics will fade. Character and integrity and**
> **really making an impact on someone's life,**
> **that's the ultimate vision,**
> **that's the ultimate goal—bottom line.**
> —Ray Lewis

Allow your thoughts to be joyful for those that have found happiness, financial success, or career success. These are often the people that you want to spend time with, as they will challenge you to grow. Discover what you admire most, and make sure that you uphold the same standards for yourself.

Some of you may reach your thirties and decide that you do not have time for new friendships, or spending time with new people. I encourage you to challenge this thinking and make time for those who you admire. Reach out to them. Find your common ground. Be a friend first.

Be honest with yourself and with others.

As you age, the relationships that you have with people may evolve. Through the years, however, having solid relationships, especially with other women, can be incredibly fulfilling. Striking common ground with a friend regarding your fears or beliefs is a powerful feeling. Strong connections with others create meaning and fulfillment. Find the people that you admire, and make time for them. Be a friend to them, and you will learn from them.

CHAPTER SEVENTEEN

Don't Be a D'bag

How you make others feel is important,
and that is what your legacy will be.

While the number of incredible women in the pro field certainly outweighs those that have questionable integrity, there were a handful of flawed characters in the mix. Regardless of the profession, school or circles with whom you interact, there will always be a few bad eggs. It's a shame that these are often people that stand out in your mind.

In my early days of professional racing, I used to refer to the vocal and condescending women as the "mean girls." My first National Level race, Tour of the Gila, as a Category 2 rider for Steamboat Velo, I was certainly out of my comfort zone. Several of these mean girls fed off of my vulnerability and inexperience. They screamed profanities at me as I attempted to grab water bottles from *their* team directors, "those aren't yours, b*%^&."

Presumably, I should have waited for the lone volunteer in the neutral zone as my one shot at avoiding dehydration in the race. Quite frankly, at the time, the etiquette of survival did not cross my mind. I simply needed water. Looking back, when I actually was on the big teams, with endless supplies of food and water at my disposal, I had a hard time understanding why any racer would be stingy about other racers having the essentials.

Getting screamed at in races became the norm in my early days of racing, but I never felt comfortable with it. I found myself in the lead group of ten races during one of the stages at Tour of the Gila. "What are you even doing here?" one of the top professional mean girl racers chided me. Her snarky comment implied that because I did not race for a professional team, because I did not have teammates, because she did not know who I was, I did not belong. Yet, she and I were in the exact same lead group. Those "mean girls" on the top teams, I've concluded, had their own insecurities and found pleasure in picking on the underdogs.

As I raced for better teams and my skills and experience improved, I never heard from those girls again. As with any job or sport, there will be those that act in such a way that you cannot understand where they are coming from? Were they not loved as children? Did they never learn manners? An insightful colleague always reminded me that

> **We were so fortunate to be strong women, using our minds and our bodies to reach a goal.**

when someone acts in a manner outside of the globally accepted code of respectfulness, something is happening with them internally. Their behavior, in other words, is not about you: it is about them.

Fairly new to professional racing, I incorrectly assumed that the team would *always* supply the race food. In my defense, we had a nutrition sponsor, and race food had been provided at the previous races in which I had participated. El Salvador was not an ideal country to learn this critical lesson on preparation. There was literally no race food available for purchase in the entire country!

I had a teammate who knew that I did not have race food in El Salvador. She knew that I was attempting to survive on race bottles and soggy, sticky "sandwich balls" that I mustered together. Combining the only ingredients that I had access to, i.e., white bread, sugary peanut butter and some sweetened fruit paste (pretending to be jelly), I rolled together a sandwich ball concoction. Needless to say, the sticky bread ball did not hold up well in my jersey pocket during the three hours of dousing myself with water and sweating profusely, and eventually became slimy bread glop.

This teammate witnessed me literally vomit, in the middle of a team recap meeting, as I attempted to replace calories with a warm yogurt beverage combined with a few scoops of recovery powder mix. Perhaps the combination of the sandwich ball mush and the vomiting inspired her "generosity."

Three days into racing, she offered to *sell* a few race bars to me because she had a huge bag of them. While I appreciated having proper race nutrition, and likely would have mortgaged my house to buy them if necessary, I did feel taken advantage of. If the roles were reversed, I'd like to think that I would have offered racing food to all of my teammates, at the outset, to ensure that we would have the essential nutrition to even complete the race.

When others' behaviors seem unreasonable and completely out of line for what is socially accepted, I try to maintain character. Although never easy, I do my best to:

1 Kill 'em with kindness: and

2 Recognize that this is likely not about me, but about an insecurity that is happening with them.

In the case of the teammate, I thanked her for "saving my life" with the nutrition bars. I understood that she must have been living with her own issues to wait for a few days and then sell them to me.

When bike racing situations were challenging, it was easy to lose perspective. The truth of the matter that I had to keep coming back to is the fact that we were so incredibly fortunate to have the opportunity to race bikes for a living. We were so fortunate to be strong women, using our minds and our bodies to reach a goal.

> **Be more concerned with your character
> than your reputation, because your character
> is what you really are, while your reputation
> is merely what others think you are.**
> —John Wooden

take away

Play fair. Be nice.

Maintain character and integrity.

Don't be a douchebag. How you make others feel is important, and that is what your legacy will be.

It is my firm belief that with very few exceptions, we all inherently know the difference between right and wrong. You will be wronged or treated unfairly on multiple occasions throughout your life. How you react to that situation is how your character is revealed. Hold yourself accountable for your actions. Be honest with yourself and with others.

Be happy with others' success. Do what you can to assist in their success. Jealousy is the most pointless emotion that exists. Try to keep in mind that there is room for all of us to be successful. Do you lose sleep over your colleague who was promoted before you or who makes $10k more than you? Do you stew over your friend who has the perfect husband or the nicer car or the better vacations?

There is plenty of happiness and success for all of us. Define your own.

Remember that you do not know what others are thinking or feeling. You are not in their shoes. Your colleague might yearn for the friendships that you have developed and would trade her promotion or salary for your balanced lifestyle. Your friend might admire your relationship with your parents or sibling even though she has a strong marriage. She might admire your staycations more than her own lavish trips. Do your best to be grateful for what you have and feel good about what others have. There is plenty of happiness and success for all of us. Define your own.

Being on your best behavior when you're in the steady state of life is likely an ace in the hole for you. You have no issue being kind, thoughtful, respectful when you are not under stress. Your well-behaved, sweet-talking self may have a sharper edge when put into an unfamiliar or challenging situation. The person who you aspire to be might be replaced by the sharp-speaking, negative-thinking individual.

Now, this may not happen to you, but you are aware of the type. You have witnessed the demise of self-control and the shift in behavior, if not in yourself, then in others.

My challenge to you is recognize when you are sliding down this path, and to take hold of your thoughts.

My challenge to you is recognize when you are sliding down this path, and to take hold of your thoughts. Your emotions of anger, sadness, disappointment, jealousy may not be altered. Your thought process, however, is completely within your domain. You can choose to steer your thoughts toward something positive.

I have to repeat that line, because it is so important. You are in full control of how you react when something happens to you. You are in partial control of the outcome based on your reaction. No matter how stressful, chaotic or challenging a situation, remain composed. You will be thankful in the long run— and most likely the short run, too.

> **Furthermore, you have control of how you react when handed a big sh** sandwich.**

As your emotions run wild and your thoughts deep-dive into an ocean of negativity, you still have the line to reel in your thoughts and drown the negative ones.

For the most part, it doesn't feel good to lose your temper or to react in an immature or volatile fashion. It certainly doesn't feel good to have people witness your tantrums. These are the episodes that will remain in their minds for a long time, if not indefinitely.

Identify the characteristics that are important to you to be a friend, a spouse, or a daughter. Although many pieces create the puzzle of integrity, a good starting place is to abide by the following:

1. Do what you say you're going to do.

2. Uphold the same standards regardless of anyone watching or not.

3. Be honest—tell the truth.

Make a vow to yourself that you will uphold these standards to the best of your ability, regardless of the pressure that you feel. Before reacting to a crisis, pause and breathe and find your inner control to ensure that you respond in a way in which you are proud and that upholds your standards of integrity.

CHAPTER EIGHTEEN

Hold Tight to Relationship Circles

Circle of Trust

Identify a small and select group of trusted people who know you, inside and out, who will ensure you are on track and with whom you will share your vulnerable moments.

I was fortunate to have a very strong network of trust with my husband, my family, and a few close friends. When team relationships were strained, or I felt like I was failing at racing, or I did not make the roster for a certain race, my husband, sister, and parents were the critical safety net that I had to reassure me and help me keep everything in perspective.

My sister, Carrie, continued her intuitive sibling role as a reliable and loyal navigator through the tangled web of decisions, frustrations, or doubts. She became an absolute expert in women's professional cycling and knew all of the teams, the racers, the results of the races. There were times that I finished in the pack and didn't know the race outcome. I would get back to my phone and have texts from her: "Tough day for you? Great day for Vanderkitten!" She streamed the races or followed them on Twitter. She became the communicator for my less technologically savvy family members. She became my trusted outsider with all of the insider information. She intuitively struck the balance of offering support and encouragement while remaining grounded and realistic. When considering retiring, my sister sensibly walked me through all of the pros and cons, recapping the history, reminding me of my original motivation. I relied on her insight in every major decision that I made.

When visiting Carrie and her family in San Francisco, I was delighted and surprised when her kids (aged two, four, and six at the time) recited the names of my teammates with ease, discussed the upcoming race schedule and understood what bridging, attacking, and a leadout meant. They simulated a race finish via Striders and 16" wheeled bikes. They flew down the sidewalk, throwing their arms in the air and proudly calling out their favorite racing names. "I'm Miranda Griffiths!" Anna screamed. "I'm Alison Powers," Henry yelled. "I'm Amy Charity," William announced. My heart overflowed.

Similarly, my parents learned everything there was to know about bike racing. My mom and step-dad incorporated annual road trips to Silver City, New Mexico and Redlands, California three years in a row to watch the Tour of the Gila Stage Race and the Redlands Cycling Classic.

Enjoying the funky New Mexico town, they met fans, read race bibles and drove to each viewing point to watch their thirty-something daughter fly by with eighty to one hundred female racers. They cringed as they stood on the first corner of the Redlands criterium, famous for the 180 degree turn. My mom still talks about the sound of the brakes, wheels, and profanity screamed by the highly-energized competitors. She remarks on how fast some of the women railed the corners looking as if their inside knee would hit the ground. My parents offered that comforting familiarity—treating me to a meal and a couple hour respite from the intensity of the stage race.

Although not what he may have envisioned for my career trajectory, my dad also embraced my cycling career with obstinate devotion. My race schedule displayed prominently on his calendar, he cleared his schedule to attend as many races as possible, including Sea Otter, Nationals in Chattanooga, Philadelphia International Cycling Classic, Tour of California, and Tour of Tuscany (in Italy!).

He studied the results, watched my performance, and gave endless encouragement. Dad loved nothing more than meeting and spending time with my teammates, and treating us to a meal after the end of a stage race. Observing from an insider's perspective, he often rode in the team car following the race from just behind the peloton. He generously threw himself into my new career demonstrating an unimaginable level of support and love.

Had Matt not been at the race, I would have finished last. I finished first.

My husband—who arguably had the most difficult situation in that his wife was on the road for three years—was the core to my network of trust. He did not have the luxury of time off or financial surplus to attend the majority of my out of town races. Not to mention, I had dragged him 4,625 miles away from his family and hometown of Nottingham, England (but who's counting?!) to Steamboat Springs, Colorado and then left for three years of racing. Regardless of how hard it must have been for him to live in an isolated, snow-covered mountain town on his own, he unconditionally supported my decision to race.

Our saving grace as a couple is the fact that Matt had a cycling background. Matt raced a bike before I even knew what a peloton was. Growing up in England, he raced the track, cyclocross, and the road. A natural from a very young age, Matt holds British National Titles and was on the short list for the 1996 Olympics in Atlanta. Cycling, and specifically bike racing, ingrained in every fiber of his being, created generous levels of tolerance and understanding as to why his wife might want to leave a prominent career to chase a bike racing dream.

Matt lives with an unsettled regret that he may have squandered his natural racing talent too early in his life to pursue a traditional career. He selflessly encouraged me to ensure that I did not have any regrets. Matt unwaveringly encouraged me to give it my all, knowing full well the implications it would have on him personally.

Not only did he understand my desire, he passionately and religiously followed every race, by any means possible (Twitter, texting, streaming, etc.). He instinctively became my Marketing Agent by texting, tweeting, posting every success that I had. He coined the term #prowife and to this day my former teammates still refer to me as "Amy Pro Wife."

On the rare occasion that Matt attended my races in person, he typically played a role in my success. In one of my first criteriums in the Pro 1 and 2 field, Matt observed my distracted, nervous, timid racing behavior. I sat on the back of a forty-person field, cautiously avoiding crashes or even getting too close to any of the racers. I did not know how many laps we had left in the race, and my clouded head only processed reactive, defensive maneuvers.

As we came up the back side of the course, I saw an impassioned, animated, jumping, screaming, arm-shaking Matthew Charity. "AAAMMMMMYYY," he bellowed at the top of his lungs, "THIS IS THE LAST LAP!"

Something about his intensity and his passion snapped me out of my fog. I looked down to discover that I had been racing in the small ring—

in hindsight, an outrageously newbie mistake! I shifted to the big ring, put my head down, and pedaled harder than I had ever pedaled before. I caught the riders just in front of me, passed the main peloton, caught the lead group, and had a drag race with the girl who had been led out by her teammates. To my absolute SHOCK, I passed her on the line and won the race. Matt, running to the finish line to see what happened, caught the final second. He threw his arms around me. Had Matt not been at the race, I would have finished last. I finished first.

These episodes continued throughout my racing career. Matt knew racing and he knew me and my potential better than anyone. He felt the same emotions of pure joy and crippling heartbreak that I did with race outcomes, arguably to an even stronger degree! He was invested in this journey as much as I was.

The role he played in my racing was more than "active" and almost a participant in terms of how he studied the races and racers, guided me, understood my shortcomings and how they could be improved. To say Matt was instrumental is an understatement. Matt was the single biggest contributing factor to my ability to even delve into professional racing.

Matt, my sister, and my parents were the behind the scenes army that made bike racing a reality for me. They proved to be my domestiques, the self-effacing team members essential to the success and yet received little glory or recognition. It is with some reflection that I begin to understand the magnitude of their overall contribution. I will go down saying that if I had to boil the entire bike racing experience down to one word, it would be relationships.

Circle of Success

Surrounding myself by those that were engaged in the cycling world became critical. Frankly, goals, motivation, adaptation, perseverance, and grit would not have mattered if I didn't get help along the way. Relationships are everything in this sport … and in life. Ask for help when you have those relationships established.

I was fortunate enough to live in the same state as Jack Seehafer, USA Cycling Team Director. I was fortunate enough to join a Boulder group ride, where Jack was also riding. It was a fairly small group and I only knew one other girl on the ride. We rode a total of about fifty miles with a short, challenging climb up Stagecoach, followed by a flat, fast, paceline effort through the farm roads just northeast of Boulder. The group split and at one point I was with Jack and three others. At the end of the ride, he asked who I was. I had no idea who he was!

> I continued to have this good fortune of being in the right place at the right time throughout my cycling career.

"Looks like you can climb, and you're powerful on the flats. I should get you over to Europe," Jack said to me casually.

I brushed off the comment. Had I known who he was and what he was actually suggesting, I may have quit my job on the spot! On the contrary, my response was something along the lines of: "Oh, thanks. Yeah, I love to climb. I live in Steamboat and I have a full-time job."

After relaying the exchange to my coach Jeff later that day, he brought me to my senses.

"Um, Amy, that is your opportunity to make it as a cyclist. You need to reach out to Jack and meet with him. He needs to understand that today wasn't just a good day, rather you are an incredibly strong rider. You need to understand what it would really take for you to race in Europe."

One and a half years after that initial ride with Jack, I received the email to race for the USA team. During that one and a half years, I stayed in regular and consistent contact with Jack. I kept him up-to-date on my training, and sent him my race results and write-ups. Every weekend that I was not racing, I would drive the three-hour commute to Boulder to join their Gateway Ride, for race simulation. During these rides, I would often bump into Jack who was not only observing my fitness and skill, but encouraging me to ride with attacks and ensure that I was positioned well. He became a mentor and a key figure in my cycling career, not to mention a friend.

I had some luck with timing and location, and I continued to have this good fortune of being in the right place at the right time throughout my cycling career. But what I started to realize was that this may have been more of a result of hard work, putting myself out there, and continuing to develop strong networks in the cycling community.

Circle of Experts

I discovered early in my racing career that I had to surround myself with cycling experts, including a coach and other cyclists who had similar objectives to mine.

Having a close relationship to my coach became essential. He needed to understand how I felt, when I was healthy or ill, overtrained or coming into form. It was critical that I trusted that the training plans he gave me were sufficient preparation for racing. It is easy to start to think that you're undertrained (typically at the exact time that you are overtrained) and doubt or blame your coach, i.e., the person who is managing your training and race preparation.

I literally started to blame my coach.

I distinctly remember attempting one of my challenging training sets of lactate threshold intervals. I was not able to do the intervals that my coach prescribed. Complete eight one-minute all-out efforts with two minutes' rest. By the third effort, I realized that my numbers were off by twenty percent. I could not hit the targets that he had given me, and I was less than halfway through the exercise.

I literally started to blame my coach. My thought process spiraled toward negativity, irrationally and illogically believing that I had not done enough training. I emailed my results to my coach claiming that I needed more miles and due to insufficient time in the saddle, could not complete the workout. He must have laughed reading the email. Luckily, his experience taught him that I was off my rocker! I actually needed rest.

Jeff's response to me was to take two days off of the bike and then do an easy ride on the third day. I did what he told me and bounced back to normal (with the right mindset) by the end of the week. It was critical to have an objective expert guide me when I was not able to think clearly about my needs.

While living in Tucson, having solid groups to train with every day of the week was not only motivating, but also allowed me to challenge myself beyond any limit that I had ever crossed before. I was surrounded by absolute experts in their class.

In training, I've always sought those that are stronger than me to ride with. It is undoubtedly uncomfortable, but it is what makes one stronger.

Darling, you're just on the wrong side of comfortable.

Prior to my racing career, I remember riding with my husband from Kona, HI to the Mauna Kea Resort along the Queen K Highway. We were in the last twenty minutes of a seventy-mile ride. I was riding about twenty mph on the flat road and Matt came around me and told me to hold his wheel. I was watching my speed tick up to twenty-one mph, twenty-two mph, twenty-three mph and finally twenty-five mph. My heart rate increased, my legs began to burn, and

I told him to knock it back a touch. He said, in his charming British accent, "Darling, you're just on the wrong side of comfortable."

Wrong side of comfortable? Are you mad? I'm effing dying, I thought. I will never forget the expression, or the sensation. He was right, I was on the wrong side of comfortable, and that is exactly what it would take to get where I wanted to be. Surrounding myself by those that were better than me ensured that I tested my abilities on a regular basis.

Surround yourself by the right people.

Identify the select groups that will help you accomplish your goals. These groups include your circle of trust, your network for success, and the experts. Your circle of trust are your friends, family, and mentors. These are the "tough love" friends: your family members that tell you exactly what you *need* to hear, and perhaps not always what you *want* to hear. That said, they have an unbiased outside perspective, and have your best interest in mind. It is a small and select group of people who know you, inside and out, who will ensure you are on track and with whom you will share your vulnerable moments. These are the individuals who will offer a soft landing on your worst falls and brutal honesty even when you have achieved your highest goals. These are the people who have the perspective to help you keep your thoughts and actions in check.

Your network for success includes those that have the ability to help you achieve your goals. They may include a mentor at your job, and/or a board member in a company that you aspire to work with. Get to know them, and ensure that they know you. Tell them what your goals are. Ask them for advice and keep them posted on your progress. This network will be the key to accomplishing your goals.

Finally, surround yourself by experts. Find people who do what you do better than you whom you respect, and spend time with those people (e.g., colleague/s, partner, coach, mentor). See what trades you might be able to make with those individuals. Offer to bake for them, look after their kids, or share your expertise from a different area. Be creative in how you can have a reciprocal relationship and continue to learn from these experts without feeling like you are taking advantage of their time. Be a sponge when you are with them. Ask them probing questions on how they learned their skill. Surround yourself by people who have found success in your area of interest.

Seek people who may strongly determine your success and stay in direct, personal, continuous touch with them.

CHAPTER NINETEEN

The Secret to Luck

"May I Borrow Your $10,000 Bike?"

*Angelo was the key to opening the door
to my first Professional Cycling Contract.*

In 2012, walking by a local bike shop in Steamboat Springs, I paused, lured by the glistening carbon machine taunting me from the other side of the glass. The Wilier Time Trial bike on display had the same effect as the fabled sirens, luring sailors with their intoxicating sounds.

My intention was to continue walking, but with the State Time Trial Championship just two weeks away, I had to at least take a closer look. With its sleek aerodynamic shape, disc wheel, unmistakable Campagnolo components, this time trial bike epitomized the ideal speed machine. Although I hadn't been in that particular shop often, and did not know any of the employees, the proverbial sirens were beckoning me. I had to satiate my curiosity of who it belonged to, how many thousands of dollars

> Hey, do you think I could borrow that bike for the State TT Champs in July?

it cost, and if there was a shot that I could somehow, in some way, just have the opportunity to ride that beautiful bike.

Still surprised by my brazen behavior, I walked into the shop and asked, "Hey, do you think I could borrow that bike for the State TT Champs in July?" Taken aback and amused, the guys looked at each other and chuckled.

"I doubt it," the salesman behind the counter said to me, incredulously. I'm sure he was trying to understand if he had actually heard the question correctly.

"Actually, the owner of the bike is about the same height as you," the other employee teased. "Call him."

I took the number and, knowing absolutely nothing about the owner of the bike, dialed the ten digits.

"Hello, this is Angelo," a man answered in a strong Italian accent.

"Hi, um … I saw your bike in the window at Ski and Bike Kare and was wondering if I could borrow it for a race? I understand that we're a similar size. I think I have a pretty good shot at winning the race," I rambled.

"Who is this?" he asked.

"I'm sorry. I forgot to tell you my name. It's Amy, Amy Charity. I live in Steamboat. You can look me up … on Facebook or Strava or ask the Steamboat Velo guys about me," I rambled again.

He told me he would call me back. Apparently, he reached out to "references" such as Strava and a few other cyclists in town. I heard back from him two days later.

"Yes, Amy, you may borrow my bike."

Angelo and I worked together to get the fit right on his Wilier Time Trial bike, and I was able to race the State Championships on the lightest, fastest racing machine that I've ever experienced. Not only was Angelo the owner of this beautiful time trial bike, he was the President of Wilier USA. Angelo became a riding partner, a race supporter, and a dear friend. Furthermore, he was the key to opening the door to my first Professional Cycling Contract. It turned out that Wilier was deep into conversations with Vanderkitten Racing as the 2013 bike sponsor. Angelo spoke highly of me to Vanderkitten's Team Director and a new door opened down the path of professional racing.

I'm Lost!

Tucking that critical life lesson into my back pocket, I recognized how many doors open by simply asking. My second breakthrough in professional racing also stemmed from a simple ask. Minutes after completing a Time Trial at the BeNe Stage Race in Belgium, I could barely see straight. Light-headed and dizzy, I couldn't get my brain to function properly (actually, a fairly normal state after finishing a time trial).

Despite the small radius where all of the teams were based around the start line, for the life of me, I could not remember where the Team USA van was parked. I had a follow car during the race, but the follow car was directed off course just before the finish line, so from the finish line I had no idea where to go. I was literally within a half of a mile from where I needed to be, yet was walking my bike aimlessly in a complete daze. I bumped into Pat, team director for Optum. Although I had never met Pat and didn't know the Optum racers at the time, they were the only other American team competing in the BeNe race in Belgium. I went up to Pat, slightly embarrassed about my state and the situation.

"Hi, I'm lost. I have no idea where my team is parked."

Pat smiled genuinely. "We can figure this out."

Pat could not have been more gracious or helpful. He pulled out the race bible and found where our designated parking spot was, and then walked with me part of the way until he was sure that I would make it back to the team van. Several months later, when I was sending my resume to various racing team directors, I reminded Pat that I was the completely cracked girl from the USA Team who he had kindly directed back to the van Pat remembered me, and although I approached him at a vulnerable time in Belgium, he knew who I was and had a small glimpse that I could at least be resourceful.

> **It requires strength and confidence to ask for help.**

Not only did I send him my resume, but I also arranged to meet with him for a coffee since he also lived in Colorado. I continued to stay in contact with Pat. Although initially I was not offered a contract from Optum, the relationship that I built with Pat planted the seed that would eventually secure my 2015 racing contract with Optum.

> **Everything you want is out there waiting for you to ask.**
> **Everything you want also wants you.**
> **But you have to take action to get it.**
> —Jack Canfield

If you are struggling with which direction to go, or aren't sure of what your next steps are, find an expert who has been in your shoes before. Find someone who can point you in the right direction. Ninety-nine percent of the time, this advisor is ecstatic to help. Similarly, if someone approached you and asked for guidance in something you were intimately familiar with, you would likely be honored that you were asked and happy to help.

It doesn't hurt to ask.

Asking for help can be challenging, to say the least. It is typical to fear that a vulnerability will be revealed; or that little or nothing is known about something; or even have a weakness exposed. In reality, the opposite is typically the case. It requires strength and confidence to ask for help. As my incredibly successful brother-in-law often says to those that report to him: "This isn't a closed book exam! I want you to solve this problem. If someone else has the answer or has done it before, ask them for help!"

Put yourself out there, be vulnerable and ask for guidance or direction. You will be amazed at how much you learn and how many opportunities you create.

Put yourself out there, be vulnerable and ask for guidance or direction.

PART VI

Tapping into Your Best

CHAPTER TWENTY

Asi Es La Vida!

The Hunger Games
(Selection Camp for Worlds)

After two weeks of selection camp,
we needed some sort of bond to occur.
It's unfortunate that this positive outcome
required such a harsh delivery.

Just when I thought I had persevered as much as one human could possibly persevere, just when I thought I would rank incredibly high on any measure of a grit scale, I was faced with a challenge that put El Salvador, Tuscany, and the Spring Classic European racing to shame. No example, in my three years of racing, stands out more than selection camp for racing the team time trial at the World Championship.

I can safely say that there was nothing in my life that I wanted more than to compete in the World Championships. Among cyclists, Worlds is often considered more prestigious than the Olympics. It is held annually at a different location. In 2015, it was to be held in Richmond, VA. Worlds was scheduled for September 20, and the seven of us flew from different parts of the US and Canada. I bid my farewell to my friends and family with hopeful realism. There were seven of us competing for six spots on the team. I was the alternate. All things being equal, I would be the one sent home the day before Worlds and my six teammates would compete. Although six of us had won the National Championship, my teammate, Maura, was recovering from broken ribs (crash in Qatar) during Nationals. So Maura wasn't able to attend the selection camps or compete in Nationals. Yet our director considered her high potential for the six-person squad for Worlds.

In jest, I referred to selection camp as The Hunger Games. Little did I know how real that description would feel after the ten-day period of hashing out our strengths and weaknesses to decipher the best six among seven very strong cyclists. Our team put endless hours, days, and weeks into preparing for the Team Time Trial. The previous year Optum came in fourth, just off the podium by a fraction of a second. In 2015, our goal was to be on the podium, and we had a realistic shot at getting there.

I've included the daily emails that I sent to my family, coach, and a select few friends. It's an *unedited*, honest account of exactly what happened, blow by blow, from my perspective. Although I reached a point of complete mental and physical depletion, both my teammates and I can look back and know that we all maintained integrity throughout this character building experience.

Amy Charity
To: Mom
Re: Selection Camp, Day 1, Sept. 11

Today was fairly rough. We did 2x5km efforts and 1x15km effort at race pace. We left our host house and drove about 30 minutes to the start. We rode the 15km loop once as a warmup and to check out the course. We used TT helmets and race radios and Pat followed us in the car. I'm 5th in the lineup (out of 7), just behind Annie. I was nervous on the first one and it didn't feel smooth. The course was winding, narrow, undulating and somewhat sketchy on the descents (we're going 35+mph inches behind a teammate and in aerobars). At some point, I must have taken a pull that was too long, because with about 2km to go, I didn't know if I could hang on any longer. I managed to stay with it, but my pulls got shorter. At the end of the effort, my lungs were burning, my face was red, and I was coughing. I felt absolutely horrible! We slowly rode back to our starting point and Pat asked for a show of hands: "How many of you thought that felt hard?" Nobody raised their hands! Uh-oh, I'm in trouble, I thought, trying to maintain composure. After the first 5km, the feedback we received was that we needed to keep the pace high. Jas, Brie, Leah, and Tetrick were setting a high pace. We needed to match that pace on the front and then pull off immediately.

We began the 2nd 5km effort. As soon as it was my turn on front, Maura came around me (presumably my pace wasn't high enough). We continued to rotate through, and I was able to go around Annie at one point (although it was on a climb, and in hindsight, it would have made sense to stay behind her). At the end of the 2nd 5km effort, I actually felt better than I did on the first. I wasn't at risk of falling off the back and I didn't feel horrendous (as I did on the first one).

Finally, we were told to do a 15km effort at 15 km race pace (i.e., faster than we will do the 40km race). The pace started high and I didn't know if I could hang on within the first 5km. At one point, Pat said that Tetrick was off the back, so we were down to 6 riders. My pulls on the front were getting shorter and I was thinking I may be the next to be out of it. Shortly after, he said we were down to 5. My head wasn't functioning properly at that point, and I didn't know who was missing. It turns out that it was Jasmine. Surprising, because she is hands-down our strongest. A few agonizing minutes went by and Pat said that we were halfway through the effort. I couldn't believe it because I was convinced that we had less than 2km to go! Just as I was about to get dropped, I heard that we were down to 4 riders. That was about the moment that I completely blew. I hit the rare state where I can barely pedal. Pat was yelling at me to stay on the wheel in front. When he realized how bad it was, he even told the group to slow down for me. At one point, he even told Brie to give me a push—that's never a good sign! My HR was pushing 200 and my watts were below 100—I was toast and couldn't recover. With 1km to go, he let the other 3 finish without me. Maura, Brie and Leah finished together. I finished a few hundred meters behind and felt like death.

Not a great way to begin. The confirmed spots are Jasmine, Leah, Brie and Tetrick. Annie, Maura and I are working for 2 spots and Maura is looking very strong and Annie is strong and smooth. So…tomorrow is another day and I will give it my all.

Amy Charity
To: Mom
Re: Selection Camp, Day 2, Sept 12

Although Day 2 felt better than Day 1, the outcome wasn't great for me. We did 5 x 5km efforts at varying speeds.

The first 5km effort was at 15 km race pace. It felt fairly smooth and controlled and everyone stayed together until the finish. I felt confident because I knew that I hadn't blown myself like the first effort yesterday.

The second 5km effort was at 5km race pace. Pat was yelling in the radio the entire time to keep the pace up. At one point, we lost Tetrick. With about 1.5km to go, we also lost Leah. There was a bit of chaos in the rotation and I had trouble getting back on. Maura, Jasmine, Brie and Annie finished and I was just behind them. During our debrief, Maura mentioned that she thought I was leaving a bit of a gap. Also, Pat was trying to determine where there was a lull in the speed. Everyone said it was the 2nd half of the group (i.e. Annie, me, Maura or Tetrick), but nobody could identify if it was one person or why the pace was slowing.

For the third 5km effort, Pat pulled me out of the lineup and had me go as the caboose. I was on Tetrick's wheel. After my first pull, within the first Km, I almost didn't get back on the group. The second time I worked to get back on the back, there was too big of a gap and I tried to go around Tetrick's wheel. I thought she was done so I tried to jump onto Maura's wheel and Tetrick was able to accelerate (we rode next to each other for a couple of seconds, obviously not efficient). She eventually got onto Maura's wheel and I got behind her. At that point, I knew I couldn't repeat that acceleration too many times or I would be off the back. We finally all finished together and I was at my max and about to crack.

For the fourth 5km effort, Pat pulled Tetrick out of the mix, so we just raced with 6 of us. If felt fairly smooth and efficient and we all finished together. Pat keeps checks on time for each effort and said that the first was the fastest by 4 seconds and the 4th was the slowest. He decided to take me out of the mix for the final effort.

I wasn't part of the fifth and final effort. Unfortunately for me, it was the fastest pace by 6 seconds. Everyone said that it felt smooth and Pat was psyched and pleased with the group for stepping it up for the final one.

I'm not ecstatic about my chances. Maura and Annie are both riding very strong (arguably better than me). All I can do is keep trying. The good news is that I feel so much better today than I did yesterday. I felt fairly nauseous for the entire afternoon yesterday and even thought I might be getting sick. Today I feel okay. My spirits are up, I'm enjoying myself, and it's fun to spend time with the team.

Amy Charity
To: Mom
Re: Selection Camp, Day 3, Sept 13

I hope this isn't starting to sound pathetic, or too negative. I'm trying to explain exactly what is happening, from my perspective. Today we did 1x5km, 1x19km, 1x5km.

The first 5km effort felt reasonable. It felt like a 6/7 on a scale of 1-10. I was moved up in the line to follow Leah and liked the position. Annie followed me and that means that she sets the pace when I'm getting back on the bunch. She doesn't surge and she is fairly steady, so it wasn't challenging to make it back on the group every time. There was some chaos with about

1.5km to go and Tetrick gapped Maura and the 2 of them finished a few hundred meters behind the rest of us.

Pat had planned a technical 20km circuit, but it started to rain fairly hard and he didn't want us cornering and descending at high speeds in those conditions. He found another course that was 19km and fairly straight. Annie said she preferred to be on Leah's wheel than mine and Pat switched the order back to how it had been. Nobody was dropped in the 19km effort. The pace felt reasonable. When I got to the front, I tried to match the exact pace that Annie had set. After the effort, Pat drove up to me and asked if I had been the one who yelled "steady" (i.e., telling the group to slow down). I hadn't said anything during the effort, but wasn't sure who did yell steady. Nobody owned up to it. Jasmine also mentioned that there was a downhill section where I let the pace drop.

Pat said that we were going to do one final 5km effort and he was going to have someone sit out. All signs led to that being me. Finally, we stopped at the car to begin our 5km effort. He said he changed his mind and would start all 7, but he would put me on the caboose. Arguably that's the most challenging position because when I'm trying to get back on after my effort, Jasmine sets the fastest pace on the front. It's where Tetrick typically sits. Pat called me out saying that if I didn't manage to keep the pace up, it would be even harder when Jas was setting the pace. I did stay on for the entire 5km and so did everyone else. At the end of the effort, Pat wasn't impressed with our speed.

While I'm feeling better every day, I'm not proving to be stronger than the other 6. I'm arguably on par, but as the alternate, I need to be stronger. So, I'm still hanging in there and doing the best I can. We have an easy day tomorrow and full race simulation on Tuesday. My guess is that the final decision will be made on Tuesday.

Hoping to survive The Hunger Games!

Amy Charity
To: Mom
Re: Selection Camp, Day 4, Sept 14

Rest/recovery day

Amy Charity
To: Mom
Re: Selection Camp, Day 5, Sept 15

Hi Family,

Just a quick one because I need to go to bed. Yesterday was a rest/recovery day (Day 4). Today was full race simulation, i.e. 38km at race pace. We pulled out the disc wheels, shoe covers, skinsuits, aero helmets, race radios, trainers for warm up, etc. Pat mapped out a 38km course to simulate the distance of the World's course. I was last in the lineup again (getting back on when Jas is taking her pull). Within about 10 km Maura was dropped on one of the hills. Approximately 5km later, Annie was dropped. We started to lose Leah at one point and Pat told us to go steady so that she could stay with us. The 5 of us rode together until the end. I felt comfortable the entire race. I'm feeling better every day and felt like we were riding efficiently.

I spoke to Pat after the simulation and he concluded that it wasn't fast and that the course wasn't representative of Sunday's course (he apologized for having selected that particular route). I asked him for feedback and he said that I am one of the weaker riders technically (specifically, keeping the pace high when the course is fast or technical). He said I'm riding strong, and a "heavy" course like today suits me. His concern is that Sunday's course may not. Tomorrow we will do efforts on the actual race course.

Originally, Pat planned to send someone home early. Today he confirmed that we would all stay here until Monday. He explained that we are all part of the team that will make the result happen, even though only 6 will race. I think my odds are low, but I'm still hanging in there!

We moved from our lovely host home on Monument Avenue (1 block away from where I used to live!) to an Extended Stay hotel. If you're lucky, you've never stayed in one of these establishments. The good news is that there is a Whole Foods 5 minutes away, so we're eating well. Our soigneur arrived today, so we're getting daily massages and are well looked after before and after rides.

Amy Charity
To: Mom
Re: Selection Camp, Day 6, Sept 16

Still no decision (that I am aware of) on Sunday's team. We did 2 efforts today and neither of them felt too hard and we all stayed together for both efforts. We did a 5km followed by an 8km on the race course. We anticipated that the course would be fast and technical. I would not describe it as either. The first 10km is fast and straight. The middle of the course is rolling and the final few kilometers are climbing. We are done with hard efforts, so now it's completely out of my hands.

The best part of the day was seeing all of the men's and women's teams, follow cars, etc. BMC, Tinkoff Saxo, Boels Dolman, etc. etc. Richmond is getting fired up and is filled with cyclists. Tetrick, Maura, Brie and I went out for Mexican for dinner. It was a nice change from weighing my Whole Foods salad every night and cringing at the register.

Coffee ride tomorrow morning, and perhaps a decision…

Amy Charity
To: Mom
Re: Selection Camp, I've lost track of what day it is…

Family,

This is certainly not the email I was expecting to send you. I was just about completely cracked. Leah, Annie, and I did an easy ride this morning from our hotel. Maura, Brie, and Tetrick rode to a coffee shop and Jas rode on her own. We came back for massages and began planning our Whole Foods run. Pat sent a text that we had a team meeting in 15 minutes. We all arrived in his room, somber and unsure of the news. He handed out our new skinsuits and said that he had made the roster decision. He decided to sit Tetrick out for Sunday's race. I was in a state of shock and kept a straight face and couldn't absorb anything else that he said in the meeting.

I'm racing the fu***ing World Championships on Sunday!!

That concluded my messages to my family. None of us could have ever imagined the misfortune that would happen next. Something about hitting the pavement at thirty-four mph and seeing your teammates strewn across the road brings everyone together emotionally.

After two weeks of selection camp, we needed some sort of bond to occur. It's unfortunate that this positive outcome required such a harsh delivery.

We finally knew who would race on Optum's World Team Time Trial squad, Jasmine, Brie, Leah, Annie, Maura and me. Me! The elation and belief were still starting to settle.

The last effort was the test run the day before the race. The plan was to treat the opener ride as a dress rehearsal, including skinsuits, aero helmets, and race radios. We were to practice a five-kilometer effort to simulate exactly how we would start the TTT at the 40-kilometer race pace. We had a lead moto, and Pat, our director, and Sam, creative director, in the follow car. The first five kilometers were fast and it was clear

Unfortunately, we had the perfect storm of bad luck.

that we had some fine tuning that needed to occur with our pacing. After the six-minute effort, we settled into a comfortable pace. We planned to do the final five kilometers at race pace. The idea was to simulate the last several turns and the final section as we would complete it in the race the following day.

Unfortunately, we had the perfect storm of bad luck. The team that set out two minutes ahead of Optum on the race simulation, Pepper Palace, stood on the side of the road at the halfway mark of the course. Odd, I thought, as my eyes flicked over to the team. Most likely, my teammates' focus wavered, just slightly, with the distraction of something not matching expectations.

The second distraction occurred almost simultaneously, as our lead moto started to turn left one street prior to the actual turn. As we had reconned the course the day before, we all knew that it was not the correct road for the left turn.

Finally, at that very same spot, there was an unfilled pothole right in the middle of the road. With those three distractions at the exact moment, the first in line avoided the pothole just before hitting it, the second in line hit it and went down, and the remaining four of us hit the pavement as well. It is nearly impossible to avoid crashing when traveling at high speeds, millimeters from the wheel in front, and in the aero position (i.e., hands are on the aerobars and not on the brakes).

I was the fifth in line to fly over my handlebars. I sat on the ground with my helmet impounded, skinsuit torn, previously injured shoulder aching, and pain in my knee. It turns out that I was in relatively good shape compared to a couple of my teammates. Annie's skinsuit was torn and she was holding her arm in a way that is the universal sign for the injury that we all suspected she had. Maura's helmet was also severely damaged and her headache/concussion arrived immediately.

Damaged helmet after TTT crash. The day before Worlds 2015.

Everything about our impending race changed with the crash. Not only were we down to a total of five riders, the squad changed.

Alison, who planned to complete a five-hour endurance ride while the rest of us were doing the race simulation, received a highly unexpected phone call from Pat in the middle of her ride. "Ali, plans have changed. You're racing the Team Time Trial tomorrow. Stop wherever you are and get a ride back to the hotel. We'll meet later tonight to discuss the race plan." Luckily, Alison had only completed two hours of her planned five-hour ride, so her legs would not be completely wasted for Worlds the following day.

Social Media feeds were exploding with news about our team's crash.

I unsuccessfully attempted to accept our team's fate that interminable day. Pat sent a cryptic message to the seven of us, stating that we would have our team meeting at seven p.m. that night. An hour later, we received a message from Pat confirming what we already suspected. Annie had broken her collarbone. At that point, we weren't exactly sure who would be racing the team time trial, if anyone. In complete states of shock, each of us sat in our respective hotel room, absorbing the tragedy and nursing our physical and mental wounds.

Social Media feeds were exploding with news about our team's crash. We read Twitter feeds, press releases and even watched the local news stating that we were down to five riders and may not even start the race the following day. All of this was news to us. Sitting in my depressing hotel room, I didn't want to be alone. I went to Leah's room, and joined her for Saturday daytime TV and a nail-painting session. Upon reflection, that moment remains a demonstration of Leah's true friendship, composure, unwavering support, and maturity. I hold the memory as one of the rare silver linings in a day full of heartbreak.

The seven of us gingerly entered Pat's room Saturday evening. Our energy and even our physical appearance unrecognizable from the previous day. Annie in a sling, Maura in sunglasses suffering from a severe concussion, Brie and I with ice packs covering the swollen parts of our bodies, we eagerly listened to the revised race plan for Worlds.

Pat stoically reported the news that we would begin with five starters for the race. We were back to the drawing board with race plans. We had to determine a new order, since three of the five racers were different than plan A (no Maura, no Annie, now Alison in the mix). We damaged three helmets and had to see if there were others and if they were the right size. Brie launched into an analogy about how we should race and driving a bus. I don't remember the details. I remember getting into a fit of uncontrollable laughter and the entire mood of the room shifting with Brie's relentless positivity and contagious spirit.

The morning of the race, we rode to the Richmond Botanical Gardens where the race began. Our soigneurs and mechanics arrived hours before to ensure that every potential need would be taken care of. Our trainers, trailers, chairs, even the men's bus was available for us to use. The two-to-one ratio of staff to rider ensured that every possible need we had was met.

I got on the trainer and felt every pedal stroke in my knee. I decided that I had to push through it, recognizing that this race was the culmination of all of the training and effort that our team had put into Team Time Trial.

The result of our race didn't match the potential we would have had if we had ridden with a full team. The fact that we had all hit the deck less than twenty-four hours earlier must have had some influence on our willingness to ride within millimeters of our teammate's wheel. We went out hard in the first 5km, and struggled to find the flawless rhythm that high performing teams must master to podium in Team Time Trial. Jas, Brie and Leah were taking longer pulls than Alison and me. I could tell that Tetrick was struggling as much as me with the shortened length of her pulls.

While silence and minimal communication are standard practice during the Team Time Trial, I instinctively called out "Good job, Ali," as I rolled passed her as she got back in the line. I knew we felt the same and were holding on for dear life. With about five kilometers to go, Ali took one last turn and was off of the back. I knew that I was in for the remainder of the race at that point.

> I competed in the top event in my sport, the World Championships. I felt elated and devastated simultaneously.

After an eternity, we took the final right hand turn to finish the final kilometer of the uphill finish. Jasmine led us through the entire climb and I stayed on her wheel. With Pat's minimal comment of "hang tough" instead of "you're killing it, you're beating Boels Dolmans," we knew that we didn't have our best race. We went to the finish, heaving, slobbering, attempting to stay upright. We finished; we competed in Worlds.

It took a year of reflection to finally conclude that racing the World Championships was a success. One definition of success that helped me reach this conclusion is the following:

> **Success is peace of mind that is the direct result of self-satisfaction in knowing that you did your best to become the best that you are capable of becoming.**
> —John Wooden

Starting lineup for the Worlds' Team Time Trial in Richmond, VA. From left to right: Alison Tetrick, Amy Charity, Leah Kirchmann, Brianna Walle, Jasmine Glaesser.

The meaning of success: Only you can judge.

Sometimes inexplicably bad things happen. We all want to believe the old cliché that everything happens for a reason, but oftentimes, it's hard to identify what the reason could possibly be.

If you have ever been in a position to strive for something that you want desperately, and truly believe that it is something that you have earned, then the raw and honest account of the team selection camp may resonate with you. Tightly competitive situations, especially among friends or colleagues are inherently challenging. Keeping your head high maintaining a high standard of character are the metrics by which you will be judged.

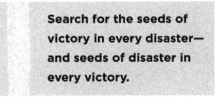

Search for the seeds of victory in every disaster— and seeds of disaster in every victory.

I've always appreciated John Lennon's quotation: "Everything works out in the end. If it's not working out, it's not the end." When something not only doesn't follow the plan, but seems to have no positive result, know that at the very least you are stronger for surviving the situation. Know that you will be able to tolerate future setbacks with a deeper understanding and strength after having been through the immediate setback. Have confidence that you will get through the situation and that it is leading you to your next phase. Finally, if you can look yourself in the mirror and know that you applied yourself to the absolute best of your ability, then seek solace in knowing that although the outcome did not match the effort, the result still goes down as a success.

Look yourself in the mirror and know that you applied yourself to the absolute best of your ability, then seek solace in knowing that although the outcome did not match the effort, the result still goes down as a success.

CHAPTER TWENTY-ONE

Was I Delusional?

Share Your Dream

The most compelling reason to surround yourself by your supporters is the argument that your reality is a direct result of your thoughts and beliefs.

Rewinding to three years before the World Championships, I believed I had a shot at racing at a professional level. With my vision in mind, I started to communicate my ambitious cycling goals to my friends and family. The responses were mixed. Some people essentially told me to keep my day job. Others nodded with a half-contorted smile. I witnessed the skepticism in their expression as they nonverbally communicated doubts that anything would ever come of what I was trying to accomplish. Some people flat out told me that I was absolutely crazy to leave a good job for a futile mission of bike racing in my late thirties. I couldn't let any of the discouragement dissuade me.

I wanted to be on a proper professional UCI racing team. Optum was my absolute dream team. I knew that my window for racing would be closing within the next couple of years and I needed to take a step in the right direction with my racing career. I sent my resume to the team director and received a straightforward response in early October 2014. In summary, Optum had filled all of their spots on the 2015 racing team. Although I was a promising candidate, there was not a spot on the team for me. The director wished me the best of luck in my cycling endeavors.

I was gutted, but remained hopeful. My backup plan, to race for a team out of Texas, would at least allow me to race all of the National Racing Calendar (NCR). I continued to put my head down and train … just keep pedaling. Stubbornly, I still envisioned myself racing for Optum, and I could not let the vision go. I truly believed that I was the perfect fit on the team.

> **My words were sparse. I could hardly breathe or form sentences.**

I knew many of the racers, I understood the team priorities, and I felt that I belonged with them. I continued to picture myself racing for Optum. I continued to train for the upcoming racing season and knew I had to just keep pedaling.

Laws of Attraction, Visualization, and Belief Actually Work!

Dear Cynical Reader, stay with me here. Just hear me out on this one.

Elated, is the best way to describe my emotional state. Perhaps *giddy* is more appropriate. I blared music, opened the windows, sang loudly and absorbed the rush of energy and adrenaline as the Arizona desert passed by. Three hours remained on my journey to Tucson for another warm weather training block. Consumed by detailed thoughts of what my 2015 cycling season would entail, the first eleven hours of the drive flew by. Energized by the phone call, I replayed every word in my mind. "Yes! Absolutely. Yes. Perfect. Done. Yep, got it."

My words were sparse. I could hardly breathe or form sentences, so communicating my acceptance was all that mattered. I danced in the kitchen with our dog Lucy, and hugged my husband, unable to coherently say the words. I had a spot on my dream cycling team.

… only the phone call, the contract, the conversation, the happy dance in the kitchen were actually just daydreams that I configured in my mind during my fourteen-hour drive to Tucson! To pass the time, or because I was stubborn, or because I found it fun to daydream, or because I actually believed that I belonged on Optum, I allowed myself to visualize how receiving a contract from Optum would look, feel, sound, and taste. As far as I knew, the eleven contracts had already been signed and there was no hope for me being a part of the 2015 Optum racing squad. Regardless, my daydream consumed my mind for the entire drive to the desert and filled me with positive energy.

Three hours later, sitting in Lynda's house in Tucson, I logged into my email. Jumping out at the top of the list of my unread email, in bold font, appeared an email from Optum's director, Pat. The first line read: *Wanted to check and see if you had solidified plans for 2015 racing season.*

OMG. This email was not a daydream. This was an actual, real email, in my inbox, from the director of Optum.

Un.be.lieve.able!

A small part of me believes that I "willed" this to happen! I responded that if he had a spot on the team, I was 100% available. It turns out that a contract with another rider had fallen through, and I was their number-one backup rider. The following day, I signed a contract for the 2015 racing season with the Optum Professional Cycling Team.

I had made it. I exceeded every one of my cycling goals and was officially a professional racing cyclist for a top team in the US.

Ten days later I flew to San Diego for two weeks of training camp in Borrego Springs, CA with my Optum teammates.

take away

Believe in yourself.

Share your dream with others. Put it out there.

Think through the areas of your life that you want to improve, and allow your mind to conjure up a clear image of your ideal scenario of what your life is like when those changes happen. Allow yourself to daydream of how your life will look, taste, and feel. Fast forward to the future you when you are in your new element having made significant changes. What does it feel like? What does it look like? Deliberately spend time conjuring up this detailed image of your new life.

Be bold and courageous by sharing these thoughts with others. Some may think you are delusional ... I suggest that you are optimistic. The reaction that you will likely encounter from your true friends and supporters is encouragement. Something along the lines of, "yes, I can definitely see you doing that. That hobby, job, activity is right up your alley." There might be a handful of people whose response is "hmmm ... can't really see it. That change will require work. Are you sure you have the skills? Are you sure you have the bandwidth? Would you really want to do that?"

Mind is the master power
that molds and makes—and Man is Mind.
—James Allen

Ensure that you are surrounding yourself with the people who are supportive of what you hope to accomplish and have your best interest in mind. If the change that you want to make is truly ambitious, some people will give you a reason that it isn't attainable. At a minimum, these are not the people with whom you want to continue to discuss your dream. At maximum, these are not the people that you want to spend time with.

The most compelling reason to surround yourself by your supporters is the argument that your reality is

Be bold and courageous by sharing these thoughts with others.

a direct result of your thoughts and beliefs. This force or power, often defined as "laws of attraction," suggests that *like* attracts *like*. Worded differently, we are responsible for positive and negative influences in our lives based on our thoughts. If you subscribe to this line of thinking—or at least do not oppose it—then guide your thoughts to actually believing that you have what it is that you are going for. This may sound far-fetched, but the mind is incredibly powerful.

You are the product of your own thought.
What you believe yourself to be, you are.
—Claude Bristol, *The Magic of Believing*
(Penguim, 2015)

CHAPTER TWENTY-TWO

The Glass Is Half Full

It doesn't matter.
You've been training well.
It was an off day.
It's not a turning point.

There were always women who were climbing better, training more, positioning better. I maintain the fundamental belief that there are no excuses and I am the one responsible for all things that happen to me, good and bad. I was baffled by those that justified their subpar outcomes. For example, after a challenging stage at Tour of the Gila, one of my competitors would send lengthy posts on Facebook about how something happened to her—out of her control—causing her to miss the essential break, and thus preventing her from winning the race. I would chuckle to myself at her preposterous delusion in her own abilities. *Had you made the break, and had a motor, you would not have won the race*, I would think to myself. Not a line of thinking that I am particularly proud of, but honest nonetheless.

As time went by, however, I concluded that I had something to learn from her positive reflection and her gentle treatment of herself. While

I'm not advocating self-delusion, or making excuses, I believe that most of us could reflect more positively on our actions. Women, especially, would benefit from acknowledging the steps we have taken to get where we are.

My coach Eric displayed this same level of positive thinking as this former competitor. I rejected his emphatic optimism in the beginning, yet learned to appreciate the value of his encouragement and even find truth to what he was saying. On my side unconditionally, Eric offered insightful and positive messages regardless of my subpar performance or less-than-stellar race results. He challenged my negative recount of my training day failures with his unflappable support and assuredness that he was not remotely concerned.

"Today's training was a disaster. I'm twenty percent low on watt targets," I told him, discouraged.

"It doesn't matter. You've been training well. It was an off day. It's not a turning point. There is no pattern of you showing a decline. Your Training Stress Score is good. We're still on track to have you do your training tomorrow," he countered.

I initially thought that Eric was too positive. I thought that he didn't understand just how bad I felt on my training ride, or just how low my numbers were, or how many hours I needed to put on the bike to be on par with my competition. It turns out that Eric knew all of this, and he knew me well enough to know when I needed to continue to train despite how I felt and when I needed to back off of my mileage. He understood how to keep perspective when I had an off day. Every athlete has low numbers or can't perform on certain days. This is absolutely a real phenomenon, and Eric understood this. He consistently supported my efforts and thoughts through continuous positive reinforcement and encouragement.

From Alternate to National Champion

Not only was Eric positive about my training and racing low points, he fundamentally believed that I was one of the strongest riders, even on the Optum Team. Having joined the team as the "last pick" or the "first pick on the waitlist," I joined with subdued confidence. Eric, on the other hand, would have none of it. He believed that the team was lucky to have me, and they were lucky that they discovered someone with my strength to join them. A complete shift in mindset. Eric planted the seed with our team director, Pat, that I should be one of the members of the TTT team. Pat certainly was not planning on having me as one of the TTT racers in the beginning of the season. As he observed my work ethic, teamwork, and strength, he started to consider the possibility that I was one of the stronger contenders for the team time trial.

After the Individual Time Trial at Redlands, I received a text from Pat that he needed to meet with me that afternoon. I had absolutely no idea what he needed. I assumed that it was a general conversation about the upcoming stages of the Redlands Race. Pat came over to the host housing where I was staying and informed me that

I could barely sleep that night due to my excitement.

I would be part of the team for the Time Trial racing Nationals in two weeks. In absolute shock, I almost fell off the couch. He told me that I had performed well at the Individual Time Trial in Redlands that day and it was the final measure that he needed to make his decision. I can't recall anything else that he said to me that afternoon because I was in a state of pure elation. This selection was beyond my wildest dreams. I was still getting used to the fact that I was racing for Optum. I could barely sleep that night due to my excitement.

An absolute far-fetched dream had come true. I was racing with one of the strongest teams in the country in the National Championships for the Team Time Trial.

The stars aligned with the help of my coach believing in me, and putting the idea out there that I should be considered for the Team Time Trial. They aligned with me believing that I was one of the strongest racers for this event. Hard work, belief, positive thinking and my dream became a reality.

> "Hard work alone will not bring success.
> The world is filled with people who have worked hard,
> but have little to show for it. Something more than hard work
> is necessary: it is creative thinking and firm belief in your ability
> to execute your ideas. The successful people in history
> have succeeded through their thinking.
> Their hands were merely helpers to their brains."
> —Claude M. Bristol, *The Magic of Believing* (Penguin, 2015)

Pleasantly surprise yourself.

take away

Believe in what you are capable of doing. Believe that you are doing what you need to be doing. Be gentle on yourself, which is the most challenging. Being a competitor, it is especially difficult to reach your own standards. There are always faster, smarter, braver competitors out there, so being the "best" can feel like an unattainable goal.

With that in mind, continuously remind yourself of everything that you have accomplished. Think through where you were before embarking on the journey of change. Review your old goals and remind yourself how far you have come. Everything in your life has led you to this point. Be proud of what you have accomplished. Know that despite any setbacks or perceived inadequacies, that you are exactly where you need to be at this moment. Do not go down the rabbit hole of self-deprecation of what you haven't accomplished. Redirect your thoughts, when necessary, to ensure that you are acknowledging and rewarding your progress and your successes, that are relative only to you.

PART VII

Reflection

CHAPTER TWENTY-THREE

The Good Life

Overcome with hope, excitement,
and pride, I walked through
that lobby, not even attempting
to suppress my enthusiasm.

Walking through the race headquarters in the Heavenly Mountain Resort of Lake Tahoe, I struggled to maintain a calm composure. The tranquil hotel lobby transformed into women's cycling's version of the Red Carpet before the Oscars. Media conducting interviews of the Who's Who in bike racing filled the lobby with the buzz of German, British, Australian, and Dutch accents. Matching the noise was the sheer movement of handshakes, interviews, hugs, and stretches of racers entering and exiting the lobby.

Each individual, pacing in and out of the hotel lobby, had a story and a specific reason for attending the Tour of California. Cycling Legends Paul Sherwen and Phil Liggett, for example, scouted out the race favorites, hoping to have a brief catch-up prior to that evening's pre-race dinner and team presentation. Their final preparation involved gathering tidbits that they would use when introducing each rider on every team. Having watched these two cycling personalities for years, it was surreal to know that in a few hours they would call my name and welcome me to the stage.

> **The Tour of California subsumed every experience that a female bike racer dreams of.**

Paul and Phil were two of the many cycling celebrities milling around the Lake Tahoe headquarters the day before the race.

With focused and serious expressions, the mechanics rolled pristine carbon racing machines into the bike area, fully understanding their critical role in the bike racing equation. Not only did the bike need to sparkle with cleanliness, races could be lost if the bike was not dialed into perfect working order. With a job of similar importance, the chefs and nutritionists from Skratch Labs understood their role in providing nutritious and balanced options catered to a highly demanding group of vegan, celiac, vegetarian, dairy-free, low-fat, or high calorie women. Team directors, soigneurs, fans, family members, and sponsors created the infectious energy of the room.

Overcome with hope, excitement, and pride, I walked through that lobby, not even attempting to suppress my enthusiasm. The feeling I had walking through that lobby enveloped all that I had worked toward, aligning in one perfect moment. Reveling on the weekend of bliss, the pros on the bike racing scale shifted ever so slightly to outweigh the cons.

The Tour of California subsumed every experience that a female bike racer dreams of. Optum brought the A team, both staff and cyclists. Our media director, mechanics, team director, and soigneurs ensured

> **Take a step back and think through your successes. Go out and celebrate everything that you have accomplished.**

that every need was met. My entire family, including nephews and my niece, clad in their best orange Optum attire enthusiastically cheered on my

Race preparation: soigneur applying embrocation on my legs for warmth. Endless Cliff products for fuel. Teammate (National Canadian Champion) Leah Kirchmann, nephew William, niece Anna, and dad.

teammates and me to create the cumulative racing experience that I had only dreamed of.

The last road race in which I ever competed was the Colorado Pro Cycling Challenge. The Pro Cycling Challenge encapsulated every dream and goal I had related to road racing. It was a stage race (my favorite type of race), in Colorado (my favorite state and home state), in Fort Collins (the town where I grew up and parents still live), over Rist Canyon (one of my favorite climbs), with my dream team (Optum), my favorite race number-22 (the number I chose for all sports), and just about every important person in my life in attendance. For this opportunity alone, every tradeoff was worth it.

Amy on the finish line of her last road race, the Pro Challenge in Fort Collins, Colorado. Photo credit: George Fargo

take away

Enjoy the ride.

Often the natural tendency is to focus on making improvements, or to think through what did not go as you expected or as you planned. Take a step back and think through your successes. Go out and celebrate everything that you have accomplished. Identify a milestone and really give yourself the acknowledgement, credit, and praise for what you have done. To the degree that you're comfortable, let others know about your successes. Relish the moment and the feelings of gratitude that you took a chance. Relish what you've learned, what you have become, and what you have experienced in your journey.

**I know of no more encouraging fact
than the unquestionable ability of man
to elevate his life by conscious endeavor.**
—Henry David Thoreau

CHAPTER TWENTY-FOUR

It's Worth It

I took a chance,
learned more in three years
than I ever thought possible,
and fully lived.

Now you know, Dear Reader, based on the spoiler in the title. At the age of forty, with eighteen plus months of reflection, I assert with unwavering conviction that my decision to do a trade-off every existing comfort in my life to become a professional cyclist was absolutely worth it. With my career at the hedge fund derailed, my Steamboat Springs relationships on hold, my bank account dwindled, my personal gains outweighed all of these losses. I took a chance, learned more in three years than I ever thought possible, and fully lived.

Throughout my cycling career, especially in stage races like El Salvador, or the agonizing months of the unknown, during heavy rejection periods like the fall of 2014, or after a broken bone, separated shoulder or concussion, or during the height of emotional challenges of being away from my husband for extended periods, I asked myself why I raced.

I concluded that it's hard to rationalize bike racing. It's not lucrative. The fame is only among those of us who ride. The act of racing isn't comfortable, not to mention the endless hours of training regardless of the snow, wind, heat or any other condition that Mother Nature sends our way. It is highly dangerous with many factors completely out of control of the cyclist. Furthermore, the esteemed look of cyclists (emaciated upper bodies, gaunt faces, bulging veins, powerful thighs) isn't exactly aligned to mainstream's view of beauty. Bike racing as a career is unreliable, as teams, races, sponsors, and racers come and go every year. "You are only as good as your last race," is a belief that permeates into racing cyclists' daily thoughts. The sport embodies suffering and hardship on many levels.

> After spending three years of my life consistently on the wrong side of comfortable, I can look back and say that I lived, I took a chance, and I followed my passion.

With all of that in mind, the racer makes a conscious decision that the rewards outweigh the obstacles. Despite all of the risks and downsides, bike racing delivers an unmatched euphoric high. After spending three years of my life consistently on the wrong side of comfortable, I can look back and say that I lived, I took a chance, and I followed my passion.

Cast your mind back to the original vision that I described as I was simply dabbling in the thought of taking my passion to the next level. The scene, existing only in my head at that point, described the deafening crowd lined up five people deep for the final mile of the finish line, my celebratory gesture, and the feeling of euphoria.

> It has never been clearer to me that the greatest rewards and the highest level of fulfillment come from overcoming the biggest challenges.

Now that very image exists. Not only engraved in my head as the original vision, but also captured in photographic evidence that I will carry proudly for the rest of my life.

Amy's Vision. Pro Challenge finish, Golden, CO. Photo credit: George Fargo

My sister, niece, parents (all four), best friend from childhood, former teacher, boss, and husband were all in Golden, CO supporting me in my final road race, along with thousands of cheering fans. While some of

the details aren't the same as my vision from years ago (I didn't exactly win this particular race!), the euphoric high and moment pride is exactly what my dream was all about.

Amy Charity after final race, Pro Challenge in Colorado. Fans: Reese and Quinn Barry.

In Conclusion

If there is one message that you take away from this book it would be that it is never too late to follow your dreams. It is never too late to find something that makes you feel alive. Our tendency is to get stuck in the routine and monotony of our lives, and to eliminate discomfort. I challenge you to do the opposite—embrace the discomfort.

> **Whatever it is that gives you goosebumps and gets you excited to get out of bed in the morning (in addition to coffee), follow that lead.**

Follow that lead with tiny millimeter steps until it is within reach, or follow it with reckless abandon. Regardless, take action to get yourself there. Visualize what you want to do, have confidence that you are on the right track, and have the belief that you are competent.

Start somewhere. Do something. Make a change now. You are capable. Your life, to date, has prepared you for what you want to achieve, but you have to start somewhere.

> **Let everyone else call your idea crazy ... just keep going. Don't stop. Don't even think about stopping until you get there, and don't give much thought to where "there is." Whatever comes, just don't stop.**
> —Phil Knight

To be clear, there is a price. There is a price with every risk that you take. There is a risk every time that you put yourself out on a limb, and wish and hope and strive for something new. Know that that risk of stepping outside of your comfort zone is a necessary step to getting to the next level.

> **It is never too late to find something that makes you feel alive.**

Chase your dreams and allow yourself to be on the wrong side of comfortable. Confidently know that you are leading a life that you will never have regrets.

Develop relationships with friends, partner/spouse, siblings and parents. Strive for rock solid, mutually reciprocating relationships. Graciously and whole heartedly share what you know, encourage those that are on the top or bottom of their game to make improvements and be their best. Humbly accept support and help and encouragement from others. From the halfway point in my life, it appears that these relationships are the nuts and bolts of a happy and successful life.

> **Your work is to discover your world
> and then with all your heart to give yourself to it.**
> —Buddha

While I haven't completely resolved the ultimate question of what is life all about (nor is there universal agreement that this quotation actually came from Buddha!), I support the simplified notion that finding one's purpose or interest and dedicating yourself to it is certainly one undeniable piece of the equation.

Glossary

Block 1 – A term used by USA cycling to define a period of time and specific races that the national team will compete in Europe. There are 4 blocks and each takes 6 riders to race.

Category - The division of racers based on ability and/or experience.

Campagnolo - A revered Italian manufacturer of road components and wheelsets founded by Tullio Campagnolo in 1933.

Caravan - The motorized "circus" that accompanies most major professional stage races and even some amateur events, the caravan is composed of officials' vehicles, motorcycle police, team cars, medical vans and photographers.

Criterium - A mass-start race covering numerous laps of a course that is normally about one mile or less in length.

Cycling Kit – Clothing that cyclists wear that include shoes/socks, helmet, sunglasses, jersey, and gloves.

Disc Wheel - Used for an aerodynamic edge, mostly in individual races against the clock, like time trials and triathlons, these high-tech wheels feature closed construction making them disc-like and super slippery so they slice through the wind for free speed.

Domestique - A French term for the riders who support their team leader in the race. A domestique's goal is not to win the race for themselves, but to help their team leader win by protecting the leader from wind, chasing down attacking riders, etc.

Echelon - A form of paceline in which the riders angle off behind each other to get maximum draft in a crosswind.

General Classification (GC) - The overall leader board in the race showing each rider's total cumulative time in the race.

Grinta – Italian for grit, drive.

Motor Pace - To ride behind a motorcycle or other vehicle that breaks the wind.

Paceline - A group formation in which each rider takes a turn breaking the wind at the front before pulling off, dropping to the rear position, and riding the others' draft until at the front once again.

Palmarès - French for an athlete's list of accomplishments.

Peloton - The largest group of riders in a road race, also called a pack or a bunch. Why stick together? Riding in a pack allows cyclists to take advantage of drafting, saving them some much needed energy during long races. Peloton is French for "platoon."

Primes (pronounced preems, after the French word for "gift" often incorrectly spelled "premes") Intermediate sprints within a race, usually offering a prize and/or points. Prizes can be cash, merchandise, or points, depending on the race.

Recovery Ride - An easy ride where one makes an effort to keep heart rate and power to low levels to assist in flushing out and restoring the muscles.

Road Furniture - Features in the road intended for driver safety such as roundabouts, traffic domes, steel covers, all which become hazards to cyclists in an open road race.

Road Rash - The scrapes and brush burns you get from crashing on the road.

Strava - A social network that connects athletes by "posting" workouts to a shared site where the athlete can review and compare workouts.

Team Director - Responsible for managing almost all logistical concerns of the racing team he/she is in charge of. At the highest levels of cycling, during races, the directeur sportif drives behind the peloton watching live race coverage on a dashboard mounted TV and informs his team on proper race strategy via radio. He may also pass out drinks and help with medical or mechanical issues.

Team Time Trial (TTT) - Instead of an individual rider, whole teams set off along a specific distance at intervals. It is a spectacular event because the teams go all out on the most advanced aerodynamic equipment and clothing available. To maximize the slipstream advantage, the riders ride nose to tail as close to each other as possible. With the riders so close together, going so fast and at their physical limits, crashes are common. Some teams targeting an overall win practice this event with rigor and the result is a beautifully precise fast-moving team that operates almost as if they were a single rider.

Time Trial (TT) - Also called the "Race of Truth." Each rider competes individually in a time trial, racing against the clock. Each rider begins alone, followed by another rider thirty seconds to one minute later. Riders can pass each other on the course but they are not allowed to draft off of each other.

Trade Team - Team sponsored by a commercial entity.

Union Cycliste Internationale (UCI) - The world governing body of bicycle racing, headquartered in Geneva, Switzerland.

Watts - The unit of measurement for power, or the rate at which energy is used over time. The more power applied to the pedals, the greater the wattage. A more common cycling unit of measurement is watts per kilograms (or watts/Kg); it takes the power to weight ratio of a rider into consideration.

Wilier Triestina – High end bike manufacturer, over a century old, that sponsors several world-class teams by providing their top-of-the-line bicycles.

World Championships (Worlds) – Considered among cyclists to be the most prestigious race in cycling, the UCI world championships are annual competitions promoted by the Union Cycliste Internationale to determine world champion cyclists. They are held in several different styles of racing, in a different country each year.

Photo Gallery

Mom and Amy at Redlands

Tour of California. Dad, sister (Carrie), nephews
(Henry and William) and niece (Anna).

Champagne Celebration of the Steamboat Springs Stage Race, 2014. Breanne Nalder, Amy Charity, Abby Mickey. Photo credit: George Fargo

Amy racing the spring classic race in Belgium, Omloop Het Nieuwsblad, "in the gutter," 2015

Amy in the final kilometer of the Big Bear Time Trial, Stage 2 of the Redlands Cycling Classic 2015.

Amy interviewed prior to Colorado Pro Cycling Challenge 2015.

Matt, Amy, Dad after final Pro Challenge race.

About the Author

Amy Charity's motivation in life has always been to live without regret. With this driving force behind critical life decisions, coupled with an upbringing focused on education and career, she has teetered on a path of a corporate career and passion-driven focus. Graduating from Vanderbilt University, she developed the skills necessary to thrive in a corporate culture and became an essential foundation that led to a decade in the financial field. As an athlete, an Ironman, endurance trail running and finally cycling consumed her time outside of the corporate workplace.

In four years, Amy dramatically morphed from a manager at a hedge fund to a professional cyclist on the US National Team, signing a contract with one of the top ten women's professional racing teams in the world. Her team won a National Championship in the Team Time Trial and raced the World Championships.

Every time a unique opportunity presented itself, she made a concerted effort to say yes, and explore life just outside of her comfort zone. One consistency in her life has been resilience.

She lives in Steamboat Springs, Colorado with her husband Matt and their dog Lucy. Each summer, she brings cycling camps for kids and adults to Steamboat Springs.

https://www.amymcharity.com/

Working with Amy Charity

Amy Charity's life is inspiring—full of risk taking and certainly living on the wrong side of comfortable. Amy has a unique background with 15 years in the financial sector from banking, venture capital and a hedge fund. At the age of 34 she left the financial industry to pursue her passion and a career in professional bike racing. Amy raced for the US National Team, holds a national title in the Team Time Trial and raced in the World Championships. Her story is one of taking chances, doggedly chasing dreams, having a vision and perseverance, and living a life without regrets.

Amy's humorous and engaging style immediately captures the audience's attention with unique and entertaining tales from the pro peloton and on corporate teams. The twists and turns in her stories are bolstered by meaningful insight and lessons learned. Every talk is designed to inspire tangible action. She compels the attendees to consider their personal boundaries, and challenges them to step outside of their comfort zones to discover untapped potential. Her experiences deliver an intense understanding of teams and doing the impossible.

Learning Objectives
- What it takes to be a National Champion
- Motivation, grit, perseverance, mental toughness
- What separates the good from the great
- Getting past uncomfortable
- Confidence and overcoming fear of failure

Amy is bilingual: English and Spanish

Contact Amy at:

Amy Charity

AmyMCharity.com/

255 Caribou Lane

Steamboat Springs, CO 80487

970.215.4045

Follow Amy on:

 Facebook: *https://www.facebook.com/amy.charity.1*

 LinkedIn: *https://www.linkedin.com/in/amy-charity-4a3b5a/*

 Instagram: *https://www.instagram.com/amymcharity/*

 Twitter: *https://twitter.com/amymcharity*

Grinta Cycling Camps

GrintaCamps.com/

GrintaCamps@gmail.com

Steamboat Springs, CO

Follow Grinta Cycling

 Facebook: *https://www.facebook.com/grintacamps/*

 Instagram: *https://www.instagram.com/grintacamps/*

 Twitter: *https://twitter.com/GrintaUltra?lang=en*

Acknowledgments

I am forever grateful to those who helped pull this book together. To Sam, for planting the seed, over a decade ago, suggesting that I might have a story to write. To mom, doggedly plowing through every chapter, every-single-time I had an update. To dad & Kathy for filling my bags with articles on perseverance and books on writing, grammar and storytelling; and for thought provoking conversations ensuring that I was on the right track. To Dave, for his old-school style of clipping and mailing WSJ articles to keep me on point with cycling stories. To Carrie, for relentlessly asking for updates to ensure that I made progress. To George, for his creativity and passion for photography, and for generously and patiently capturing training and racing images. To Judith, for her no BS style to get it done. Finally, to Lucy who was literally by my side, every day, in her oversized bean bag occasionally forcing my hands off the keyboard when she wasn't getting enough attention.

Writing this book allowed me to retrace the steps of my journey and absorb the monumental contributions that my family, friends, team-mates, coaches had on my ability to even embark on this adventure.

To Kyle, for reading the maps, helping to keep my bike in working order, and for igniting the spark that launched this entire journey.

To Jack, Angelo and Pat for taking a chance on me. You took a risk on an unknown and opened opportunities that would otherwise not have been possible.

To Carrie, for your loyalty, encouragement, and honest, straight forward delivery. I hit the jackpot having you as my sister (and best friend).

To mom, the most patient human on the planet—you exemplify what it means to be nurturing, and supportive. You set the standard for being a mom.

To dad, my next book is an ode to you. Nothing I could write would begin to do justice for your love, support and generosity. I strive to emulate your strong character and pray that at least some of your traits are passed down to me genetically.

To my coaches Jeff and Eric, for teaching me to train with purpose and intention, for challenging me to test my limits, and for believing in my potential.

To Lynda, for feeding me, housing me, and keeping me entertained with endless laughter.

To my teammates, for showing me the modern world of social media, for exposing me to Netflix classics such as Gossip Girl, for being my family away from home, and for patiently teaching me how to be a racing cyclist.

To Matt, for his wit, way with words, seeing the world from a unique perspective, for challenging me to get on the wrong side of comfortable, for embracing a life a long way from England, and for being a keeper.